SECONDHAND STYLE

Sonya Mills

AURUM PRESS

ACKNOWLEDGEMENTS

My thanks to all the people who helped me to write this book, especially Tony Byers of The Electricity Council; Leslie Durham of Oxfam; D. A. Grimes of the Oxfordshire Trading Standards Department; David Havenhand of Johnson Wax; Gillian Roth of Maidstone College of Art; Paul Viney of Phillips Auctioneers; Phyllis Cadman, Christian Fraser and Arthur Cooper.

Published by Aurum Press, 33 Museum Street, London WC1

ISBN 0 906053 55 2 (hardcover)

ISBN 0 906053 41 2 (paperback)

Illustrations by Peter Bolton

Cover photography by Jon Stewart, by kind permission of Great Expectations

Designed by Neil H. Clitheroe

Phototypeset by Bookworm Typesetting, Manchester

Printed in Great Britain by Hazell Watson & Viney Ltd, Aylesbury, Bucks.

CONTENTS

INTRODUCTION

Why buy secondhand? To save money, certainly, but for many other reasons too. It's a way to acquire beautiful and unusual things not found in every other house in the land, or on every other person's back. It offers hours of fun browsing through the incredible variety of goods on offer in street markets, auction rooms, jumble sales and dingy shops with come-hither names like Second Chance, Chameleon or Serendipity. You can buy things which, being well made in natural materials, you could not afford new: silk, not synthetic fibre; solid wood, not veneered chipboard; leather, not plastic; silver, not base metal stamped out in Taiwan. Then there's the glow of achievement that comes from restoring battered furniture to use and beauty, bringing dead electrical equipment back to life, cunningly adapting and altering clothes. You can enjoy the battle of wits over prices: getting a dealer to part with an over-priced item at a sum *you* are prepared to pay, not what he had visions of prising out of some innocent (who has not read this book!).

Above all there is the pleasure of exercising and developing your taste, your nose for the pearl hiding among the tat. Pearls may be few and far between, but these days even a bargain oyster is worth having.

I must make it plain straight away that I am not talking about antiques. Once something is classified as such it acquires snob value and its price rockets. I am not interested in buying anything merely *because* it is old. If I buy a secondhand table it's got to be cheaper than a new one – certainly not more expensive.

Similarly with clothes. This book is not really concerned with 1920s cocktail dresses and Victorian underwear (though I have touched briefly on such items); they are now much sought-after, and therefore overpriced. I am talking about the vast tide of discarded modern clothing. People do not throw things out only because they are worn but for other reasons too: they have increased a size or two since last year; the wretched thing never did suit them; they are the kind of person who *must* have this year's fashion. Wearing secondhand clothes used not to be at all the thing, but now it's amazing how many affluent-seeming ladies, complimented on some item of dress, will happily admit to finding it at a jumble sale, and boast of how little it cost.

Buying secondhand is a must for the young couple setting up home on a tight budget, with most of their money disappearing in mortgage, rates and heating bills, not to mention luxuries like food and drink. Such buys fall into three categories. Stop-gaps, like the secondhand fridge you hope will keep running until you can afford a new one; items to be relegated, like a warm but hideous carpet that will be moved to the third bedroom as soon as possible; and finally treasures, the lucky buys which you may keep and enjoy all your life.

It is for this group of secondhand buyers that I have included a chapter on household equipment, for here big savings can be made now that even a basic new cooker costs a three-figure sum.

Tableware too is always in abundant supply and, once you abandon the notion that place settings must match, you will probably be able to collect practically everything you need for the table – china, glass, cutlery – plus useful kitchen items like carving knives, fish kettles and preserving pans.

Many secondhand items – silent clocks, broken china, ancient flat irons and umbrella stands – seem quite useless. But to the cultivated eye for attractive shapes these can become unusual household ornaments. Some discretion is needed here, or you can get carried away – I have in mind the stag's head in the loo, the milkmaid's yoke on a town house wall. But dammit, if *you* like it, anything goes.

Other good secondhand buys are items originally made for a particular purpose which you can use for something quite different, either just as they are, or by adapting them.

Finally the big stuff: secondhand fixtures and fittings. Many Victorian or Edwardian houses have been denuded by insensitive former owners of many of their original features. Replacements can usually be found if you know where to look; but prices are often unreasonably high, as demand has become great and dealers grasping. So you need to go shopping well primed with knowledge.

Which is what this book is all about. To help you spot the treasures that lurk among the junk without spending for ever over it – secondhand shopping is fun, but can be very time-consuming. To teach you something about how to pay the right price, and not get ripped off. To give you some guidance on where to look and how to operate – auction room rules are different from those of the jumble sale. And finally to show you how to make your buys look better than new, through your own skills. No expensive equipment or special tools are required unless you get badly hooked on furniture restoration, and even then you can hire what you need.

I have been buying secondhand, on and off, for the last twenty-five years, sometimes out of necessity, as when furnishing my first home entirely from London junk yards. For fun, during more affluent periods, I have bought secondhand bric-a-brac, silver and chinaware. Again out of necessity, during those times so common in the lives of full-time writers when bills fly in faster than cheques, I have been back to the secondhand shops to keep clothed and shod. Some of these buys were treasures and are with me still. Others were never meant to last, and the few disasters are easily forgotten, as I never pay very much for anything. It has given me a lot of fun and saved me a lot of money. I am sure it will do the same for you.

1 FURNITURE

At first glance much secondhand furniture looks pretty unappetising. Never mind; you are looking for *potential*. It's rather like buying a house. You don't buy it for the way it looks with the incumbent's hideous floral carpet fighting floral curtains, floral wallpaper and lurid paintwork; you have a vision of how delightful it will be when you have finished working on it. Sometimes you will be lucky and happen on something reasonably priced that you like as it is, or that needs no more than a good clean. But most items will involve at least a little restoration and repair work.

So you need to cultivate an eye for the eventual looks of a table or cupboard when cleaned of treacle-brown varnish; a kitchen chair freed of umpteen coats of chipped paint; a sagging, balding fireside chair after re-upholstering. This means you are looking for furniture with good basic shapes. Paint and varnish can be stripped off, peeling veneer stuck back, superfluous mouldings removed and legs and handles changed, but the basic design is for good.

Pieces that qualify have been made at all periods, and so have hideous ones. In a large secondhand emporium or at an auction you will see items made over several centuries, with a preponderance of those from the nineteenth and twentieth. Discounting the genuine antiques (made before 1830, when machine manufacture got going), which are too expensive unless on the verge of collapse, that gives you the products of the next 150 years to choose from, during which time styles changed enormously.

Because it was so well and solidly made there is still a lot of late Victorian and Edwardian furniture around, much of it large and made of mahogany, with fancy inlay work. I have not personally come across much furniture of the twenties and early thirties, with its angular lines, imaginative use of the new invention, plywood, and chromed steel. Perhaps its owners are still cherishing it. What you do find are reproduction Jacobean pieces: massive sideboards and tables with elephantine legs, overly endowed with carving and funereally stained to counterfeit seventeenth-century oak.

Then there is a large group of what I term 'landladies brown' – the sort of dingy cellulose-varnished wardrobes, tables and chairs found in bed-sits everywhere. This kind of furniture has been churned out for a very long time – and still is. Though it is never very exciting the older pieces may be solidly made and will provide serviceable storage. As it is so neutral and you need have no qualms at mucking it about, it provides a good basis for transformation scenes (see Chapter 6).

Much of the furniture made just after the Second World War is soundly constructed and remarkably good-looking in its way. Next we are into the spindly splay-legged furniture that screams 'Festival of Britain 1951', and that is due for a new vogue any time now among the trendy set. After this things start to deteriorate. The styles of the fifties linger on and on, getting more and more debased. The veneered chipboard, plastic laminate and vinyl 'leather' era has arrived. The trouble with a lot of this newer furniture, even if you like the style, is that it was often so cheaply made that it is falling apart. Also the manufacturing methods used can make it very difficult to repair or recover satisfactorily.

Some furniture is virtually timeless, and there are items which have proved so popular that manufacturers keep churning them out more or less unchanged. Among these are Windsor chairs, bamboo ('rotten banana') tables and wicker chairs. Pine furniture, too, comes under this heading. This was originally cheap stuff used to furnish cottages, kitchens and maids' bedrooms in grand establishments. Its age can range from very old to made yesterday, but as it has, ironically, become so desirable and remained so for such a long time, it is now highly priced almost regardless of age, condition or style. These days you will find it difficult to catch such items before they have been dipped in a tank of hot caustic soda and whipped into a trendy shop with a three-figure price tag attached. Any you do find are likely to be heavily painted, but

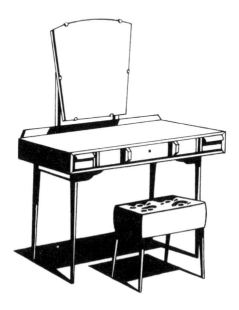

if you are prepared to work on them yourself (see page 19) your reward can be great, or you can always cheat and send them to a stripper.

Chests of drawers are the commonest items likely to come your way, plus cupboards and shelf units of various sorts and kitchen tables (so-called 'pine' chairs are more often made of light-coloured hardwoods). Sorry, but you are most unlikely to find a Welsh dresser you can call a bargain, even the most dilapidated one. But you can always fake your own (see Chapter 6). Other things not to expect on your treasure hunts are a chaise-longue, a four-poster bed or a love seat. But you can always live in hope ...

A lot of the furniture on offer is genuinely of its period, but many of the older pieces are likely to be reproduction. The Jacobean 'oak' for example, will not be genuine, and many Victorian and Edwardian styles have been reproduced copiously. An aged appearance is no guide. You must know that there are people who make brand new 'antique' furniture look old by 'distressing' it. My father did this for a time. His work involved lashing furniture with chains, gouging it, bashing it and jumping on it in hobnailed boots. He found all this far too violent and went into the Second World War. But if, like me, you are buying secondhand simply as a cheaper way of furnishing your home, this need not concern you. It is just useful background knowledge to have when you are pricing an item. If a dealer thinks that you believe a piece to be genuinely old he will bump up the price. Unless you are really expert you can never be absolutely sure, whatever he says. But once you make it plain that you are not interested anyway, but just want a cheap item to furnish your au pair's bedroom, you are in a much stronger bargaining position.

What to buy from this motley mixture? I find that pieces from most periods will mix happily together, but you may decide to specialise in one. Some people like to keep to a particular wood in the same room – all pine, all oak, all mahogany. If you are lucky enough to have large high-ceilinged rooms you can display to advantage the larger items such as Edwardian wardrobes or 'Jacobean' pieces, and you should find them relatively cheap as buyers for them are few.

Bamboo, cane and wicker furniture is lightweight and gives a summery, outdoor feel to a room. Very plain 'basic brown', stripped and painted matt white, can masquerade as bang-up-to-date. As for pine, you either love it or loathe it. Its former great virtue, that of being dirt cheap, is rapidly disappearing. And I should tell you that pine really is a soft wood, and gets badly dented in time. But I still love it for the beautiful golden colour that develops over the years, and the whirly grain and knots that make other woods look dull.

Whatever your views on styles it's as well to set out with some idea of what you need, otherwise you may be tempted to buy all sorts of nice things that just clutter up the house. But never close your mind to the unexpected bargain! As in any ordinary shop, about 90 per cent of what you see won't interest you anyway: you don't like the style, it's too expensive or, in the secondhand world, it's too decrepit in relation to your willingness and ability to restore it.

This last is an important point you should always have in mind. Suppose your heart is set on a balloon-back chair. One in good condition, needing little work beyond cleaning and polishing, will probably be quite expensive. One that needs re-upholstering you might consider; but one with a broken joint in the back frame, and a wobbly leg indicating trouble there too, calls for much more skill and time to put right. In the following pages I will be giving some clues for spotting such common faults, to prevent you being lured by a bargain price into buying a load of trouble. Even if you are highly skilled and undeterred by the prospect of hours of labour to restore your prize, knowing how to spot faults that others might miss puts you in a good position to haggle over the price. And, of course, *never* admit that you intend doing the work yourself. Imply that the price must take into account the vast cost of paying a restorer.

Before we look at the various items of furniture likely to be on offer, a quick word about woodworm. This is a very misunderstood animal, and wrong advice is frequently given about it. I am in a position to give you the lowdown, because I once worked for Rentokil. My first job each morning was to open dozens of little packets containing dead creepy-crawlies sent in for identification by alarmed householders. The main thing to grasp is that a scattering of small neat holes in wood shows where the adult beetle form of the woodworm left for the great outdoors, not where the worm ate its way in. Therefore, more worm may or may not still be actively tunnelling around inside; to be safe you should assume that it is. Some people are so terrified of woodworm that they won't buy anything showing a single hole; others happily ignore them and are surprised when more turn up in woodwork all over the house. I would not recommend buying a piece so badly eaten that parts of the wood are soft and crumbling (always look at the back, as the pest prefers unpolished wood). But if the wood is sound it is quite safe to buy – as long as you treat for woodworm, and not by blocking up the holes after the beetle has bolted. See page 122 for the proper methods.

Woods and veneers Much of the charm of old furniture is that it is made of interesting woods, some of which would be prohibitively expensive today. Mahogany, fine-grained and rich reddish brown, is common in Victorian and Edwardian pieces. Oak, light yellowish brown, sometimes with flecks in the grain, was widely used for dining tables and chairs. Beech, pale, speckle-grained and sometimes pinkish from having been steamed, was the common stock for stick back chairs; for better quality ones yew was often used, which has wild, wavy grain and colour which can change, over quite a small piece, from dark brown to buff. What is loosely called pine, or deal, can be one of any number of softwoods, all with pronounced grain and frequent knots, ranging in colour from almost white to reddish brown. Exotic woods used for more expensive furniture include rosewood, very dark with pinky-purple tinge; ebony, which really is black (but often counterfeited by 'ebonising' other woods); burr walnut, rich brown with a rosette-like grain and bird's-eye maple, pale blond and dotted with 'eyes'.

Often the more expensive hardwoods were used in the form of thin veneers glued on to a cheap groundwork. There is nothing wrong with this provided it is still hanging on reasonably well and not splitting. Some of the most priceless antiques feature decorative veneers, and even quite ordinary items may have doors with four veneer panels laid so as to form a mirror-image pattern.

Tables It is easy to fall for a table that's far too big for a small modern dining room; secondhand furniture has a nasty habit of looking smaller than it really is in a big auction room or warehouse. So always check size with a tape measure. A 150cm (5ft) long table seats six comfortably; if you plan large dinner parties go for something that folds. Oak draw-leaf tables are quite common; you might even get matching chairs like the ones on the front cover. For a really tiny room look for drop-leaf tables, which fold down into a very narrow space. The gateleg type in oak or stained beech should not be too expensive, but Pembroke tables, where the leaves are supported by brackets, may be dear, particularly if made of mahogany. Circular-topped pedestal tables of all kinds are highly desirable, but consequently not cheap, and often in poor condition – wobbly and with a split top. (They are not easy to repair.)

Old kitchen tables with deal tops are often in appallingly insanitary condition, but if the frame is sound and the price low it's a simple matter to fit new boards to the top. For an authentic look they should be left unvarnished; plane off the sharp edges and ends to get rid of the brand-new look. Small side tables with a couple of drawers and shallow backboard are handy items and also make useful desks. Large marble-topped wash stands can be turned into tables by removing the splash-back, though this does tend to leave a mark behind.

Chairs Secondhand chairs are great fun to buy because there are so many totally different styles. Single chairs are always cheaper, pro rata, than sets, so it makes sense to build up a collection of non-matching but compatible ones (to go with your collection of non-matching but compatible tableware – see Chapter 3). Depending on the style of your other furniture, and general decor, look for sturdy stick backs and oak dining chairs, delicate bedroom and drawing room chairs, balloon backs with plush seats, or reproduction Chippendale. Bentwood chairs fit in anywhere, but are no longer cheap; bear in mind that brand new ones can be bought for about £30. (New bentwood rockers cost about £70.) Cane chairs of any kind are often available cheap because they need recaning, which is quite expensive, not because it's highly skilled work but because it takes hours. So if you are one of those lucky people with time on your hands you're laughing. Any craft shop should be able to supply caning materials and a booklet explaining the basic technique (see Useful Addresses, p.126).

Bauhaus-style tubular chromed steel chairs with leather sling seat and back are not terribly likely to turn up outside of Sotheby's, but if they do, your price guide is that Habitat have various new chairs in this style for £50-£60.

Old deck chairs can be a good buy, especially the more elaborate ones with arms and/or foot rests; replacing rotted or missing canvas is a simple job. New ones, basic style, with nasty plastic instead of canvas, currently cost about £7.

Another useful buy for small homes are folding chairs, the kind used in church halls, as they provide guest seating which can be stored away in between times.

Conventionally made chairs, with legs jointed on to the seat, get put under terrible strain during long years of use and misuse, so always check the joints before buying. Push and pull the legs to detect any undue waggle, and look under the seat for signs of botched repair work, such as rusty nails and angle brackets.

Upholstered furniture Before buying any kind of sofa or armchair check the springs, by the simple process of bouncing up and down on the seat, and feeling all over for suspicious hard lumps. Next assess whether the covering is liveable with; if not the cost of recovering, making new loose covers or

buying stretch ones will put the price up considerably. Also check size; some old sofas are on the vast side, although there are also plenty of small two-seater, cottage types around. Some old sofas are designed so that one arm rest can be let down, which is nice for relaxing or sleeping. Full-blown bed-settees of ancient manufacture may be suffering from rust in an already cumbersome mechanism; opening out *and* closing up is recommended. Also lie on them; some are back-breakers.

Beds Bedding manufacturers would much rather people didn't buy secondhand ones, hinting darkly that it's very risky as *you don't know where they've been*. Well, they would, wouldn't they? But precisely because lots of people don't fancy them secondhand, beds can be very good buys. Really old ones are bound to need a new mattress (possibly base as well, depending on type) soon if not straight away, but can be well worth buying for the head and footboard alone. (You can forget about old brass bedsteads – they are now collectors' items, out of our reach.) I still have a beautiful mahogany bed with inlay work and mother of pearl decoration which I bought many years ago for £10, which very soon became the price of a new headboard.

Bounce on beds as on sofas to check the springs, also to find out if they are embarrassingly noisy. With old-fashioned double beds, as opposed to divans, find out whether they come apart, otherwise they may be incredibly difficult, and sometimes impossible, to get upstairs. Always inspect mattresses on *both* sides, as even a pristine-looking modern divan may have something to hide.

Storage furniture Down the years cabinet makers and factories have produced so many variations on the basic chest and cupboard that you should have no trouble finding something that provides the storage space you need, pleases your eye and is not too expensive. A chest can be anything from plain whitewood to over-priced pine to walnut veneer with brass swan-neck handles. A sideboard might be a thirties one in bird's-eye maple, a solid pseudo-Jacobean production or a low elegant teak one dating only from the early sixties. Wardrobes range from vast mahogany numbers to minute brown-varnished or whitewood boxes. A dressing table might be dark and elegant with swing mirror and jewellery drawers, or white and kidney-shaped with rococo-style gilt mouldings.

Old cabinet furniture has often been given replacement knobs and handles, often in quite the wrong style, and can be greatly improved by fitting something more appropriate. More modern stuff often has fancy ones also best replaced with something plainer. Over-decorated items covered in moulding can easily be modernised by stripping it all off. Ugly legs can be removed or replaced with modern screw-on ones.

Heavily painted items are always of interest, however terrible they look, as the wood beneath might turn out to be not boring whitewood or ply but some beautiful hardwood. With tables and chairs it's fairly easy to guess from the style what wood lies beneath, but small cupboards and the like are totally anonymous once painted. Inspect chipped paint closely to see what's underneath and if necessary take a penknife for a discreet scrape when the dealer is not looking. Such furniture should be cheap because you face all the labour of stripping it.

Wickerwork, rattan and bamboo Wickerwork chairs were traditionally used to furnish conservatories and verandas, but they make good cheap indoor furniture, except that they do have a distressing tendency to ladder ladies' tights. Inspect seats carefully to see that they are not sagging and close to breaking point, as they cannot be satisfactorily repaired.

Similar, but of softer, finer construction are rattan chairs. Do not get carried away and pay too much for these; a new rattan armchair in traditional style can be bought for about £30. Even finer articles are Lloyd Loom chairs and sofas.

These are not made any more and are highly collectable; also very comfortable.

Bamboo tables, although they look frail, are very durable, so there are still quite a lot of old ones about. They make good bedside tables or pot plant stands. To my mind they look better left with their natural 'rotten banana' appearance than painted. Nearly always the covering on the table top and shelf below has been replaced with something dreadful, often sticky-backed plastic, and can be transformed by fitting new grass cloth. See Useful Addresses for mail order supplier.

RESTORATION WORK

The ideal secondhand furniture buy needs no more than a clean and polish when you get it home. Other pieces will need to have a tired finish revived and minor repairs carried out. Those you buy dirt cheap will almost certainly need stripping and refinishing, and more extensive repairs. But these can be the most satisfying, provided you actually manage to finish the job. (I must own up to two half-finished projects in my garage, and a chest in the bedroom which has been in use, half-stripped, for so long that it's never going to get finished now.)

On the other hand you might get hooked on furniture restoration as a way of life. It happens to some – you have been warned!

Start by removing any fittings that come off, for cleaning separately, and to make the main item easier to work on. If rusty, painted-in screws refuse to budge apply penetrating oil and wait until they ease. Unless it is obvious that stripping will be necessary, give the piece a good clean. Then do the repairs, if any. Junk furniture is often damp, so if drawers or doors are sticking just leave it alone for a few days to dry out and the problem may magically disappear. (Furniture restorer's motto: *nil exertum necessarium* – never do any more work than you have to.) Lastly do the reviving or refinishing work.

Cleaning

If your acquisition is made of superior wood such as mahogany, or is veneered, do not set about it with hot water, detergent and a scrubbing brush, however filthy it be. This will ruin the treasured patina, loosen joints and lift veneers. Make up a mixture of 4 parts white spirit to 1 part linseed oil and rub it on with a coarse cloth pad. This will shift dirt and old wax without disturbing the finish below. Fine steel wool (not the kitchen kind filled with pink soap; buy a roll of 000 grade) is permissible to winkle dirt out of nooks and crannies, but don't rub too hard – the change of colour around moulding or carving is one of the things that gives an old piece its character. Pine, painted furniture, bamboo, cane, and wicker pieces can all safely be washed, but take care to rinse off detergent with plenty of clean water and dry the objects thoroughly – out of doors is best. When a painted item is to be stripped there is little point in washing it first unless it is thickly coated with grease (*nil exertum...*). If it just needs repainting and is not filthy a time-saving approach is to wash it down with liquid sander, a product that simultaneously cleans and prepares the surface for repainting.

Clean tarnished brass fittings with steel wool and shine them up with metal polish. If painted dunk them in a jar of stripper. Brass inlay, or fittings like key-plates which cannot be removed, should be cleaned with a cut lemon dipped in salt as this will not affect the wood.

Vacuum upholstered sofas and chairs vigorously to remove the dust of ages and, hopefully, retrieve valuable coins from down behind the seats. Clean fixed-on fabric with upholstery shampoo. Grease spots should yield to spot remover, but a large patch on the back of an armchair where some gentleman's heavily oiled head has rested for years is there for good. Old loose covers are safest dry-cleaned in case they shrink. Or if they look to be rugged linen ones you can risk it and gently hand wash. Putting them in the bath and trampling with bare feet is very effective – you might even get the kids to do it for you. But do not soak, and if the fabric is patterned dip an edge in hot water first to find out if the dyes are fast. Put the covers back while still damp and iron (if necessary) *in situ*.

Wash marble with detergent and water containing a good dollop of ammonia. Stains may – or may not – yield to bleach solution; apply it all over to avoid a patchy look. Polish with silicone furniture polish, and for a terrific shine use a lambswool polishing pad in an electric drill.

Removing blemishes and reviving the finish
Don't panic if hardwood furniture looks worse after cleaning than it did before. It may well do so, because that coat of wax and dirt was concealing stains, scratches and cracks as well as giving the wood colour and shine.

Do-it-yourself books abound with weird and wonderful methods for removing blemishes from furniture. Personally I have found that many – such as steaming out dents with a hot iron and damp cloth – simply do not work, while others call for great skill and hours of fiddly work, and often end up making the blemish more obvious than before. In any case, scratches and dents are the badges of the piece's genuine antiquity – you don't want people thinking it's a modern reproduction, do you? So, provided the piece is not actually disfigured by blemishes, I find it much better simply to make them less noticeable and follow up with an all-over reviving treatment. If they are deep, numerous or large you can often just strip and refinish the affected section (usually the top); it is not necessary to do the whole thing.

White or dark rings and scratches may yield to proprietary products designed to deal with them, if they have only penetrated the surface finish. Slight (pale brown) burns can be reduced by scraping gently with a sharp craft knife, and small ink stains lightened by dabbing with bleach on a cotton bud. Fill small holes and cracks with matching wax crayon (melted in a teaspoon), larger ones with plastic wood.

After this give the finish a reviving treatment, and if necessary recoat it. A simple method of reviving a tired old finish is to rub the surface with liquid metal polish or car paint cleaner, which are both mildly abrasive, on a soft cloth. A more vigorous treatment, particularly effective on old French polish, is to use proprietary restorer and cleaner and rub it on with steel wool. This stuff contains methylated spirit, and dissolves the top layer of the finish, taking minor blemishes and ingrained dirt with it. Follow up either treatment by polishing the furniture with wax polish.

To recoat a finish you need to know what the old one is. An old, good-quality hardwood piece is likely to have been French polished. Test by rubbing an inconspicuous part with a rag dipped in methylated spirit, which will dissolve the finish and so stain the rag. Applying a reviving coat of French polish is a simple matter, quite different from building up a complete finish from bare wood. Just buy a jar of French polish and follow instructions. (French polish contains a rich brown stain; button polish is slightly more orange; for pale wood buy white polish, which is bleached.) If the test rag remains clean the finish is most likely cellulose or a modern varnish; both can safely be revived with a coat of clear polyurethane.

Fine country furniture made from elm or yew should only have a wax finish, which cleaning will have removed. Refinishing the old way with hard beeswax (which is also difficult to get) is tedious, and a similar effect can be had by sealing the wood with a thin coat of shellac or polyurethane, and then using wax polish, which contains silicones and so is much easier to buff. An ordinary beech stick chair might just as well be finished with polyurethane.

Teak furniture (and rosewood, if such exotic splendour comes your way) has an oiled finish which should be revived with a coat or two of teak oil.

Stripping

If your bargain is badly or thickly painted; has any finish that's chipped or flaking off all over; is varnished a depressing dark brown; or sporting white marks, dark rings, vast ink stains or a tasteful mixture of all three, there is no alternative to stripping the finish right off, back to the bare wood. (Be quite sure it is not a genuine antique before you start; stripping will not improve its value.)

Stripping is never fun but there are plenty of different methods to choose from, all of which have their good and bad points. You don't have to stick to one but can combine them to good effect. The three basic ways to go are: dry – abrading or scraping off the old finish; wet – dissolving it with chemicals; and hot – melting it.

To abrade a finish away you need some kind of power tool (hand sanding a complete piece would take for ever). Using a rubber pad covered with abrasive disc, fitted into an electric drill, is the fastest method, but very coarse; it is only suitable if the piece is later to be painted. An orbital or finishing sander is very much gentler, and best used to clean up and smooth the surface *after* using chemical stripper. Both these tools are only for flat surfaces. For shallow curves such as a chair back or seat a drum sanding attachment is good; this can also be used on the flat but keep it moving or hollows will develop. For fiddly pieces like stick chairs a much smaller attachment called an abrasive flap wheel is handy, as it doesn't damage the curves and can get into confined spaces.

As sanding physically removes a tiny layer of wood along with the old finish it gives a very clean, new look, and gets rid of deep-seated stains. But don't power-sand veneers – you could go right through.

Liquid chemical strippers have been around for many years. They work in a few minutes, but only on one or two layers of paint at a time. Each application has to be scraped off, which is rather laborious. The new peel-off chemical strippers work much more slowly, over a period of hours, but will penetrate ten or more layers of paint. And they really do peel off; no scraping is required, which reduces the risk of damaging fine wood with an over-enthusiastic dig of the scraper. But they are expensive. I use peel-off for high-quality woods and anything with lots of turned parts, barley sugar legs or carving, and the cheaper liquid type for junkier, plainer furniture, especially if it only has one or two thin coats of varnish. Another advantage of the liquid type is that it's safe to put it on anything, whereas peel-off can turn some hardwoods black, must not touch metal and is not recommended for veneers.

Both types are powerful chemicals, so read and follow the instructions carefully. Anything that dissolves paint doesn't do skin, eyes, clothes or carpets any good at all.

Heat methods are of limited use for furniture. The traditional blow-lamp is too prone to singe and char the wood, as well as set fire to the curtains. A hot-air blower is safe, but an expensive toy (£20) to buy just for the odd bit of furniture restoration. A third method for flat surfaces – safe and cheap but slow – is to use an ordinary domestic iron. Just set the iron to high, place it on the wood over a piece of aluminium foil and leave for a few seconds. When the finish bubbles up move the iron to a new spot and scrape the finish off quickly before it cools.

If you can't face any of this send your treasure to a commercial stripper, who will dunk it in a tank of hot caustic soda and may charge more than you originally paid for it. This is very drastic treatment and can leave wood looking dull and grey, as it removes natural oils. Do not send veneered, plywood or bentwood items to a stripping tank or they will come back in bits.

After rinsing off chemical stripper allow the piece to dry thoroughly. Fill any holes or cracks with matching wood filler, or white cellulose filler will do if the object is to be painted; if it is not and there are patches of old white filler scrape out the top of these and replace with wood filler. Sometimes, on cheap pine, you may find a layer of milky white paint sunk deep into the grain. This is almost impossible to get off completely and you may have to resign yourself to a cover-up paint job. Old wood stain can be removed with bleach (domestic or wood) or by sanding, but if some dark patches still remain give the whole piece a coat of fresh stain to even things out. Stains can also be useful if the wood looks somewhat pale or lifeless.

Finish by sanding lightly in the direction of the grain with fine abrasive paper and wiping clean with a rag dipped in white spirit.

If you want a very high gloss finish, perhaps to match a stripped section to the rest of the piece, buy an old-fashioned product called grain filler. This is a powder that is thinned with white spirit to form a creamy paste which, rubbed across the grain of the wood, fills the pores.

Choosing the new finish
The basic choice is between clear finishes, which enrich the colour of the wood and show up the grain pattern; and paint, which hides defects and gives solid colour.

Clear polyurethane varnish is very hard to beat. It's super-easy to apply and shrugs off hard wear, hot plates and spilled drinks. It can be glossy, satin or matt. If the wood lacks colour you can use a coloured polyurethane; or apply wood stain first. Another possibility is plastic coating or cold cure lacquer. This comes in two parts that have to be mixed together. It is more expensive but is very quick drying, even more hardwearing, and never yellows with age.

French polish takes time and skill to apply, and at the end all you've got is a similar gloss to polyurethane, that will be spoiled the first time someone stands a hot wet mug on it. But if you insist on trying it get a French polishing kit, which is designed for amateurs and has full instructions.

An oil finish is very light, does not do much to protect the wood and only gives a slight sheen. But it is the quickest and easiest to apply – you just wipe it on with a rag. Use teak or antique oil, not linseed oil – even the boiled variety takes ages to dry.

The best paint to use on furniture is gloss, which is the most hardwearing and has plenty of 'body' to cover defects. But if you don't want a mirror-like shine you can use a paint with a satin finish. On bare wood use a primer first to seal the pores.

Conventional gloss paints are best applied over an undercoat, but the thick non-drip kind are used coat on coat. Most of the big-name brands are now available, thank goodness, in easy-brush-clean form, which eliminates the old chore of cleaning brushes in white spirit (or in my case leaving them in a jar of the stuff until it's too late to do anything but throw them away).

Emulsion paint is not suitable for furniture as it quickly wears off on sharp edges, and pale colours absorb dirt. But if you want to paint a large item white a quick way to do it is to use emulsion and then protect it with a coat of varnish. Aerosol spray paints give a very smooth finish and are quick drying, but expensive for anything large, and the colour range is limited.

Simple repairs

This is a vast subject and I can do no more here than point you in the right direction and pass on a few tips. But old furniture was designed to be refurbished, and if you take the trouble to study the way it was put together commonsense will usually guide you. For example if the leaves of a draw-leaf table don't function, look at the underside of a healthy one. And light patches on a wooden frame often show where a vital block of wood, such as the stop that prevents a drawer from being pushed too far back, has dropped off.

A basic set of household and woodworking tools will cope with most minor furniture repairs, provided it includes a few G-cramps to hold pieces tightly together while adhesive dries. The correct tool for knocking joints apart is a rubber mallet, but an ordinary hammer serves perfectly well if you protect the work with a scrap of wood. A workbench and vice are a great help but not essential. For upholstery work get a set of upholsterer's needles – these are long and strong, and one will be curved.

A great deal of furniture repair involves gluing broken bits together again. Use woodworking adhesive (white PVA) for most wood-to-wood joins like repairing a split component. This allows you plenty of time to correct mistakes, is clean to handle and doesn't stain the work. But its drawback is that the

parts *must* be tightly clamped together while the adhesive dries. Using G-cramps is often difficult because awkward shapes are involved, or the item is too big; but string or Scotch tape can be used instead, and sometimes a weight. (Anything heavy will do – I use a length of old narrow-gauge railway track, a relic from a romance with a railway enthusiast.)

If something is really impossible to clamp – such as a missing piece of moulding – use a contact adhesive, but make sure to get the component correctly positioned quickly, as you have only a few seconds to manoeuvre. Contact adhesive is also used for gluing on sheets of veneer.

Do not expect any adhesive to work if the parts to be joined are dirty, covered in old glue, or worn away so that they no longer fit together. And although modern wood adhesives are extremely strong, you can't glue a broken chair leg together with them unaided.

Other types of adhesive you may need are an epoxy resin (two-part) for joining broken metal components; and latex and vinyl adhesives for upholstery work. Avoid the new miracle glues – they are expensive, unnecessary for this kind of work and nastily prone to glue your fingers together.

Chests and cupboards To secure loose handles, knobs or hinges unscrew, plug the hole(s) with plastic wood, matchsticks or dowel and refix with new screws. Replacement fittings are readily available from specialist suppliers (see page 126) but be prepared to go into shock when told the price of brass ones.

Sticking drawers: try rubbing a candlestick or soft pencil on the runners. This may disclose that they are deeply grooved, or that one is missing. Plane flat; or turn upside down and reglue; or fix a new one. If the dovetails at the corners are coming apart the drawer will stick because it is out of square. Remove the bottom panel, gently knock the drawer apart and reglue. Wide drawers may stick because the bottom panel is sagging – refix the centre support.

Sticking doors: probably hinge trouble. Try tightening the screws, swapping hinges top to bottom, and packing hinge recess with card. If some idiot has fitted new hinges that are too thick deepen the recess.

Chairs and tables Trouble with joints between frame and legs is a major problem, especially on ill-treated chairs. Most dining and balloon-back chairs have mortice and tenon joints, where a square stub fits into a matching hole. If they are just wobbly you might get away with squeezing in some adhesive. Otherwise knock the joints apart, clean off old glue and reassemble dry to see if the parts all fit, then apply adhesive. In both cases cramp the joints up while the adhesive dries by tying a string tourniquet tightly round the seat frame, padded at corners to protect the wood. Also check that corner braces inside the frame are all present and tightly fixed.

If you can't face this, or if the joints prove to be damaged, resort to repair plates. These are steel or brass, in four shapes: 'L', right-angle, 'T' and straight, with holes for screws. Provided they can be placed so that they do not show they can be used to reinforce or repair all kinds of joints – and even breaks, if placed on both sides.

Stick chairs are held together with dowel joints – tapered ends of components fit into round holes. These are easier to repair as no clamping is needed. But it may be necessary to knock a whole section apart in order to get one straying stick to go back into its socket.

Plain round stretcher rails on dining and bedroom chairs are also dowel jointed. If one is broken, cut it off close to the holes, then drill out the stub. In order to be able to insert the new rail despite the fixed space between the two legs, drill one of the holes out extra deep.

Legs Sawing bits off table or chair legs to correct wobbles can end in disaster, particularly when they are splayed rather than straight. I find it best to pack up the shortest leg by gluing on a bit of hardboard or something similar. Or try fitting *one* furniture glide. (Old furniture glides are invariably rusty; replace with new ones before they mark the carpet.) If you do feel brave enough to risk cutting off bits of leg the standard method is to stand the item on a level surface, insert packing under the short leg then use the packing to pencil cutting lines on the remaining legs.

Castors Old castors can be so badly worn that they no longer work freely, and replacements should be fitted. There are two basic types: cup castors, which fit over the legs, and screw castors which screw in. The latter can cause finely tapered legs to split, and if this has happened it's safer to replace them with the cup types.

Veneers Before sticking back a loose piece of veneer scrape out the dirt and old glue underneath, otherwise it won't stick or be flush with the rest. Spread on a thin coat of woodworking adhesive and weight the repair down well until dry. To repair blisters slit them to allow trapped air to escape, squeeze in a little adhesive and weight. If bits of inlay work are missing, or a whole panel is so badly split it needs replacing, new pieces can be obtained from a specialist supplier (see page 126).

Upholstery Fitting new covers to dining and fireside chairs is simple if they are just tacked on. Remove the old cover carefully and use it as a pattern for new fabric. Replace flattened old horsehair or wadding with polyether foam, and broken or sagging webbing with new (stretch this tight by pulling it over a block of wood as you tack it down). Springs in fireside chairs may need tying back into place. If the frame is peppered with old holes fill them with plastic wood to create a firm base for new tacks. Stick braid on with latex adhesive to cover tacks.

Fitting new loose covers to sofas and armchairs is a much more ambitious undertaking. It is not inherently difficult, but the cost of buying many yards of expensive furnishing fabric, worry about whether it's all going to come out right in the end, and the sheer labour of all that sewing are enough to have put me off the whole idea now that one can buy quite reasonable stretch covers. If you do decide to try it, get a book on upholstery and do an armchair before tackling a sofa.

Stretch covers are available to fit an amazing variety of quite ancient sofas and chairs. Send the manufacturers a model number or drawing and they should be able to say whether they have a stock pattern to fit; if not they may have a made-to-measure service. To look good stretch covers should be in thick material, so that the fabric below does not show through; beware of cheap, shiny fabrics. They should also not be too tight a fit, which gives an unpleasantly strangled look to the furniture.

2 CLOTHING

There has always been a market in secondhand clothing, but shops that were once discreetly named Deirdre's Dress Agency and Bingham Bros. have blossomed forth as Second Gear, Rosina's Relics, Encore and Antiquarius, making no secret of the origin of the stock. For dressing secondhand-style has become high fashion among the young, some of whom would never dream of buying *anything* new. Quote from the *Guardian* fashion page: 'Stay with the layering, the jumble of textures, the essential baggy shapelessness of the garments, the clumpy, eccentric-looking footwear beneath collapsed socks or wrinkled leg-warmers.' What better place to find such a look than on the secondhand market? (Actually you can buy it in regular shops too, because the rag trade, tired of losing custom to charity shops, is busily turning out new garments that look old, in stone-washed denim and distressed leather. But the real thing is much cheaper!)

31

Cheapness is probably the main attraction for a different group of secondhand dressers, those who no longer have as much money to spare for clothing as they used to. But so is quality: buying secondhand provides an opportunity to acquire well-made clothes in what are now very expensive materials – silk and cashmere, suede and leather – at affordable prices. And finally the sheer variety of secondhand clothing appeals to people who want to dress *their* way, rather than following the fashion of the moment.

Like other shops, secondhand ones have their own individual character. Some go in for famous names and up-market labels like Aquascutum or Austin Reed; others are into trendy gear from past decades; and some are almost antique shops, carrying Victorian undergarments and other period clothes. Some are safe and boring; others have a glorious mish-mash of everything. As in ordinary shops the quality and originality of the stock depends on the taste, energy and contacts of the buyer. So you need to find the right shops to cater for your style of dressing.

If you are the sort of person whose taste runs to expensive classic clothes, but lack an income to match, an up-market nearly-new shop can be the answer to your prayers. Look for a winter coat in pure wool, cashmere or even vicuña (South American llama wool, the ultimate status symbol), preferably with a famous label still in it for your hostess to read as she hangs it up; suede and leather jackets; tailored, fully-lined suits in tweed and worsted; well-cut day dresses; elegant cocktail and evening wear in expensive fabrics; Scottish knitwear; silk blouses and shirts; ski and resort wear; Italian leather shoes and handbags; model hats and silk scarves with hand-rolled edges.

A completely different type of secondhand clothes shop offers more of the very old than the nearly new. These are the places to hunt out slinky thirties' evening frocks in bias-cut satin; backless twenties' dresses with handkerchief hems and masses of beads or fringes; short-skirted forties' suits with square padded shoulders. These garments are in short supply so can be quite expensive, and are too precious for everyday wear. But fifties' numbers – sleeveless, shiny, full-skirted and preferably sporting a large bow on the bosom – are plentiful and consequently cheaper.

For the current street fashion, the hard times, slept-in-a-dustbin look, jumble sales and charity shops must be a prime source, if only because they are the cheapest and therefore allow the acquisition of a sufficient number of layers. Here are the shapeless sweat shirts and cellular vests to wear one on top of the other, sometimes cinched in by a broad leather belt; the long-johns to display beneath a lightweight gathered skirt, or better still two; all finished off with thick grey men's socks and

a pair of elastic-sided school pumps. Both sexes hunt for collarless shirts, trilby hats and any kind of top from which they can rip out the sleeves and cut down the neck, leaving edges ragged. Denim jackets are still in, provided the sleeves are cut off. The girls are also after large stud earrings, women's lace-up leather brogues, long tweedy overcoats with fur fabric collars and big hats to wear with a bit of fabric tied round the crown. The boys seek vast pairs of pin-striped trousers which are kept somewhat uncertainly in place with a sturdy leather belt (the more nervous sport braces as well), and even vaster greatcoats.

A different kind of scruffy look, the vaguely military, can be acquired at government surplus stores. Much of their stuff is unworn, but secondhand in that it has been sold off by the armed services of various governments, mainly in Britain, the USA, Canada and Sweden. It is rugged, very cheap, and the drab colours are highly fashionable. Here are the camouflage trousers and shirts, olive safari jackets, combat anoraks, black leather snow patrol coats, army bush jackets, despatch riders' coats, khaki shirts bristling with buttoned pockets and shoulder tabs, jeep coats and bomber jackets, macho sweaters with hard-wear patches, heavy leather jerkins, commando boots and the unisex handbag, the khaki respirator pack.

But most of us are not into street fashion or *haute couture;* we just want something to keep ourselves and our family warm in winter and cover the naughty bits in summer. At one time office workers dressed up to go to work, and dressed down at weekends: shop and factory workers condemned to overalls all week did the opposite. Now, thank goodness, things are much more relaxed, except for a few city gents and salesmen, and casual clothes are the order of the day for most activities, work or play (man was born free, but everywhere is in jeans).

For this sort of clothing the charity shops are ideal, closely followed by the kind of run-of-the-mill commercial second-hand clothes shop which has not had a rush of trendiness to the head and jacked prices up accordingly. Jumble sales are the cheapest, but quality is also lowest; besides, your need for a pair of trousers or whatever may not wait until the next one comes along; shops are open five or six days a week. Street markets, too, are beginning to sprout secondhand clothes stalls in among the purveyors of Taiwanese cheapies. I find them all good for shirts and trousers, jackets and coats. Knitwear has usually been worn to death by the time it gets into a charity shop; also shoes. Dresses everywhere tend to be on the short side, which is no good to me as I am on the tall side. Some of the commercial shops and stalls also have a line in what the rag trade calls 'cabbage' – seconds, ends of ranges and leftovers. These are unworn and you can often find some really good bargains.

Men's and children's clothes

Men usually hang on to their clothes longer than women (till death us do part in some cases), so the average offerings in secondhand shops are fairly battered – which is OK if you are into that kind of dressing. But the more up-market ones usually have a rack of reasonable suits, sports jackets and casual trousers, plus a few shirts, sweaters and shoes.

But the best place for the average man to look for a respectable type of clothing is at establishments called wardrobe dealers, which unfortunately now seem to be vanishing rapidly – the famous Kemp's, established in 1919, is one of the few left in London; a few others are listed in the Yellow Pages for Birmingham, Manchester and Leeds. In the days when all male office workers were commanded to wear suits, Kemp's did a brisk business in them, selling 150 a week. But as the suit declined they changed course and now a large part of their business is selling high-quality men's clothing to film and TV companies who prefer buying to hiring. But they still have a big range of men's wear, both new and secondhand. They use a system of pink and white tickets to indicate whether something is old or new, and everything is priced.

Most of the secondhand shops have a rack of children's clothes, which can be most useful when offspring are growing out of garments faster than money is coming in, or if you have the sort who come home from school with their clothes practically destroyed, or regularly have them stolen. But of course these are in the main casual clothes; if you have to equip the monsters with a pukka school uniform, enquire at the school, parent teacher association or school outfitters to see if any arrangements are in existence to pass on items still fit to wear when outgrown.

Avoid secondhand shoes for children: they are very bad for growing feet and responsible shops like Oxfam do not stock them. Also do not buy nightdresses. They may not have been made of flame-resistant material in the first place, or if they were its properties may have been removed by incorrect washing. And avoid any garments with a hood fastened by a cord – these have proved potentially lethal and are now banned.

Clothes for special occasions

Dressing secondhand has close associations with dressing up, and some commercial secondhand clothes shops run a profitable side line in hiring out costumes for parties, theatricals and fancy dress balls. Chameleon Clothes, in Oxford where I live, has over 800 items, which can be chosen from an illustrated catalogue as the most popular ones are rarely in the shop. Here you can hire such varied items as a union jack dinner jacket, a Babygro to fit a six-foot man, authentic ball gowns and outfits worn by TV stars.

For more mundane social events requiring a Posh Frock both commercial and charity shops can come to your aid. They usually have a small selection of long and short dresses suitable for evening wear. The smarter ones also run to accessories: shoes, evening bags and shawls. Dinner jackets are not so common unless you live in a university town, where they are popular items as the students buy them. One dinner jacket is very much like another, but with a dress there is always the nagging fear that it was handed in by someone who is going to turn up at the same function and spot you; an even worse fate than appearing in an identical new outfit as some other woman! One way of cutting down the possibility of this happening is to buy in another town, but of course that puts the cost up unless you combine the purchase with a duty visit to Aunt Maud. Another ploy is to choose a plain garment and dye it; then no one could *prove* anything, however dire their suspicions. Alternatively go for a period frock, a thirties' evening dress or fifties' cocktail number, rather than something modern.

Any no-nos?

Obviously you are not the sort of person who shrinks from the thought of wearing another's clothes or you wouldn't be reading this. But there are clothes and clothes . . . few people relish the thought of wearing someone else's underwear.

Queen Victoria's bloomers and Marilyn Monroe's bra may have been auctioned off for vast sums, but they were not exactly bought for wearing.

One exception is cotton and linen petticoats, shifts and camisoles, trimmed with broderie anglaise, lace and satin ribbons. Such items can be so thoroughly bleached, boiled and scrubbed they need not give even the most fastidious a qualm. Those sold in the smart secondhand clothes shops in Camden Passage, and on stalls in the new Covent Garden, have already been brought to a state of bone-white cleanliness. But prices are fairly high, so if you have the luck to find a tired and grubby example of the genre, snap it up and give it the works.

Nightwear also seems rather too intimate for my taste, but it regularly appears in charity shops, so someone must buy it. I prefer old-fashioned men's collarless shirts; they are soft and comfortable because so amply cut, with plenty of length to cover the bottom, and long sleeves ideal for keeping your hands warm when reading in bed. But I have yet to see a dressing gown worth buying. Not only are they worn into the ground, there seem to be only three styles, all dreadful: tartan wool no-nonsense, candlewick in hideous colours and nylon quilted or frilled, even hideouser. Perhaps better things are on offer in more up-market areas than mine: Noel Coward-style quilted satin numbers, fluffy terry cloth kimonos or Chinese dragon-emblazoned scarlet silk robes.

What about shoes? Definitely not for children, as already emphasised. And some adults would rather wear another's underwear than their cast-off shoes. They are so manifestly moulded by the shape of the previous wearer's feet that it's probably as well to avoid them if your own are at all delicate or troublesome. But otherwise you should come to no harm, though I wouldn't recommend wearing a pair for long periods standing up or going on a hike until you have broken them into your own foot shape, a precaution that applies equally – or more – to new shoes, of course. The plus point for many old shoes is that they are all leather, which is supposed to be much better for feet, allowing them to breathe, unlike many modern shoes which are all plastic.

Finally bear in mind that some of the above items may be

acceptable because they have never actually been worn, but are part of the 'cabbage' element of the stock.

Shopping techniques
Secondhand clothes shops often have a jumble of totally different styles hanging cheek by jowl, which is part of their attraction, but means you need to develop a time-saving technique to pick out anything that might be of interest, otherwise you can spend hours in them. Some people go through looking for certain colours – I once saw a glamorous platinum blonde in an Oxfam shop picking out everything red. It's as well to keep firmly in mind what the gaps in your wardrobe are, otherwise you can wander down all sorts of blind alleys, and find yourself considering the merits of clothes you have no possible use for, just because they are attractive.

As soon as you find something interesting check the size; if it's not yours forget it. Often there are no labels, and few shops put sizes on the price tags, but I find I have become very good at gauging my size by eye. Otherwise take a tape measure – shops should have one but have usually lost it. Skirt waists measure up pretty accurately; this should also tell you if the hip measurement will be OK. Measure shirts and sweaters for bust size across the back, immediately under the armholes. Fabric garments should be little larger than your actual size, to allow for ease of movement; sweaters may be a little smaller as they stretch. Gauging the length of a dress is difficult: hold it against you with the underarm seam against your own to get some idea. But if it seems likely to be short it's best to try on to make sure. Most establishments have some kind of private corner for this purpose – except of course the jumble sale, when there's no time for such niceties anyway. Trousers should always be tried on as even if the label says they're your size there are some very funny shapes around, and the legs may be too short.

Having decided that you like it, that it fits and the price is right (see notes on haggling, page 107), inspect the garment minutely. A low price may indicate some ghastly flaw. Look for stains, tears, burns, holes, split seams, missing fancy buttons, threadbare areas and broken zips. Once you have paid it is assumed that you bought accepting noticeable flaws like these. Secondhand clothes shops will not normally take anything back, as some unscrupulous folk buy things, wear them a few times and then try to return them for some spurious reason. But if you are really unhappy they may be prepared to put it back into the shop on a sale-or-return basis.

Finally, with garments like coats and suits, always assess whether they're going to need dry cleaning or not, as that adds quite a bit on to the price. Clothes are more likely to have been cleaned or laundered in a commercial shop than a charity one, and that will be reflected in the price asked.

RESTORATION WORK

Secondhand clothes may be made of unknown or unfamiliar materials that will need a little more care in laundering than the modern miracle-fibre garments you normally wear. Some idea of how to deal with a mysterious dark stain that might be anything from alcohol to zebra blood is a help. You also need to be able to tackle minor repairs, as few secondhand garments are perfect, and if you can do some basic alterations such as narrowing flared trousers your choice of possible buys is greatly enlarged.

Laundering and dry cleaning

Jumble sale clothing will certainly need a wash before you allow it near your lily-white skin, and even items from superior dress agencies who claim they always clean everything before sale often have a musty smell to be got rid of. Garments sporting a textile-care label are no problem, but many will either have lost theirs, or be too old ever to have had any such thing. Learn to identify fabrics by sight and touch. Silk is incredibly fine, smooth and warm; early imitations of it are cold and hard, more like modern man-made fibres. Pure wool has far more texture and body than wool/synthetic mixtures, and the colours are richer and more subtle. Dress cottons have a very substantial feel compared to modern polyester/cotton, and drape differently. Cotton shirting and linen feel heavy and are more coarsely woven.

When in doubt, wash any lightweight fabric in warm suds and iron when almost dry with a coolish iron, turning the heat up if this has no effect and applying steam or sprinkling with water. Deal with any pronounced stains before washing (see below). An overnight bath in biological soaking powder will remove vague stains, brighten colours and whiten whites (but never soak silk or wool, in anything). White cotton or linen that has gone yellow can be bleached after washing – use 2 eggcupfuls of household bleach in a bucket of cold water and soak until white. Ancient patterned fabric may not be fast-dyed; test by dipping a seam in hot water to see if the colours run.

To avoid sending old plain-dyed silk shirts to expensive dry cleaners, test by wetting a small corner, placing this on a piece of white cloth and pressing with a warm iron to see if any other colour comes out. If not it is safe to wash; but very gently, in a mild detergent, as for your best lambswool sweater.

Old velvet is made from silk; theoretically it should wash all right, but it might be safer not to risk anything splendid. Velveteen, however, is made from cotton and should wash as well as corduroy. But don't iron – get creases out of a crumpled dress by hanging in a steamy bathroom or playing a steam iron over it.

To wash small, delicate pieces of old lace put them in a

wide-necked jar filled with a solution of warm water and soap flakes and shake for a few minutes. Rinse in the same way and pin out to dry on a thick white towel using stainless steel pins.

Heavy garments like suits and coats must be dry cleaned, and should be quite happy in a self-service cleaning machine. It is worth sending evening gowns and cocktail dresses made of silk taffeta, chiffon, brocade, georgette and organza, and silk ties and printed scarves to a professional dry cleaner. Leather and suede coats need special treatment; make sure to pick a cleaner who knows how to handle them.

Stain removal

As the golden rules for removing stains are (1) do it straight away and (2) treat according to what made the stain, you can be in some difficulty with ancient splodges that are, as my granny puts it, 'well hittered in'. Buying something with a noticeable stain not in a convenient place to be concealed by a CND badge or an iron-on motif is always a gamble. But you should get it cheap, so if you *are* successful at spiriting the stain away your satisfaction will be all the greater. Removing a stain will usually leave a clean patch so washing or dry cleaning will be necessary afterwards.

If a stain looks greasy or oily use a proprietary dry-cleaning preparation. These are primarily grease solvents, and the paste kind is preferable as it never leaves a ring behind. Eucalyptus oil or glycerine are lubricants, and can loosen old set stains of any kind. Borax removes acid stains and should work on fruit juice or wine stains (dilute 30g borax in 575ml warm water and soak for 15 minutes). Nail varnish remover (acetone) will remove old hard varnish and many glues, but do not use on acetate or triacetate fabrics as it will attack those as well. Dried gloss paint is there for good; emulsion paint will soften if the garment can be soaked, but traces of colour may remain. Stains on white linen and cotton can be treated with bleach; and on coloured items if you don't mind a paler shade or a redyeing job. On other fabrics use hydrogen peroxide (20-vol) which is milder, diluted with 9 parts water. Iron-mould stains from rusty coat hangers, and some inks, may yield to a proprietary rust remover (from the chemist), but this is for white cotton or linen only. On other fabrics use lemon juice, then iron through a damp cloth. Methylated spirit is supposed to be the cure for ballpoint and felt-tip pen marks but they are notoriously persistent.

Repairs
Having attended to obvious faults like split seams or dropping hems, what can be done to brighten up geriatric garments? Quite a lot, even if you're about as handy with a needle as a cow with a musket. A new set of buttons can work wonders (conversely I have often bought jumble sale gear just for a set of interesting buttons). Ribbon, lace, broderie anglaise or braid trimming may be tired or torn, and can be replaced with new; large haberdashery departments have the most mouth-watering selections. Heavy sweaters with thinning or darned elbows look good garnished with bought leather or suede elbow patches; sporty jackets can be given leather bindings to hide worn cuffs as well. Worn nap on wool coats responds to a good brushing with a nap brush (or use a genuine teasel head if you happen to have a plant in the garden).

Holes and tears in other parts of knitwear can be repaired remarkably neatly provided you can get some near-matching wool – look through the piles of totally unwearable woollies that abound in charity shops and at jumble sales. Do not follow your natural instincts and cobble the edges together: proper darning is required. If this is a Lost Art as far as you are concerned exploit a granny. Holes in fabric can be discreetly patched, particularly if patterned. Steal a piece from a deep hem or the end of a belt and match the pattern or weave carefully. On plain fabrics you can also use iron-on patches from the haberdashery counter: sensible matching ones for denim and sportswear or pretty motifs and silly slogans. They also have iron-on sheet repair kits in light-coloured poly-cotton which might save a shirt or blouse.

Ancient slide fasteners noticeably lacking in zip will benefit from an application of petroleum jelly. If the fastener has come off one side, open the metal clip at the bottom with a pair of pliers, then replace fastener and clip. If the clip breaks just oversew the bottom few teeth with strong thread. However, zips like this are usually suffering from overstrain, and will eventually need replacing. This is not nearly as hard as people think, even on trousers. Remove the old zip (a seam ripper is the best tool) and buy a new one of the same length and weight. Tack this in place, open, then top stitch down each side, preferably by machine.

Men's shirts are often perfectly good except that the collars are worn along the fold from rubbing against a bristly neck. These are easy to unpick, turn over and re-stitch. The button and hole will then be on the wrong side, but this is of no consequence as you probably won't want to do up the top button anyway. Or leave the collar off; collarless shirts are highly sought-after and hard to get. To rejuvenate worn cuffs unpick the seam and turn the worn edge in; the cuff will be slightly shorter. Old-fashioned double cuffs can be cut down and re-stitched to turn them into normal ones.

De-shining the seats of men's trousers is tricky. I have seen a recommendation to use very fine glasspaper; I suppose you could *try* this on a pair of what-have-I-got-to-lose type trousers. But a good man's suit will benefit from a professional clean and press anyway, and a high-class cleaning establishment may offer a de-shining service too.

Replacing elastic that has lost its zing is another unfamiliar job these days. The secret is to thread the new elastic on a bodkin or small safety pin in order to get it through the channel. Use the same technique for slotted-in ribbons or drawstrings.

Alterations

Unless you are uncommonly short the most frequent alteration required is letting down hems on both skirts and trousers. Check before buying that there is something to let down, that the turned-under bit is not a completely different colour from the faded rest, and that the actual turn line is not discoloured or frayed. To get maximum length out of a meagre hem, simply turn under the minimum amount you can get away with and topstitch in place by machine. For a neater job, attach bias binding to the raw edge and hem under. On winter skirts and coats made of heavy material make a false hem by stitching on a band of similar-weight fabric and turning it to the wrong side.

If a skirt has nothing to let down you can gain extra length by attaching a broderie anglaise frill, or wearing it over a peasant petticoat; but of course this does rather depend on the style of the garment. Similarly a coat can be lengthened by adding a fur fabric trim at the hem, if it warrants the expense. Another dodge is to use a braid-type trimming to cover a line left by a former hem. When adding any kind of trimming around the hem area it's as well to put more elsewhere – on sleeves or neckline – to disguise the fact that it is not just there for decoration.

For those who have to take up skirts and trousers, latex adhesive is a quick and easy alternative to sewing. It stands up to washing but not dry cleaning.

Narrowing flared trousers is another essential skill. (Though as fashions change ever-faster, and tapered, drainpipe trousers are already back in vogue, perhaps by the time this book is published flares will already be in again.) It's surprisingly easy to do. Measure the width of your own favourite trousers across the bottom of a leg. Turn the flares inside out and chalk this width on the leg bottoms, equidistant from each side. Carry the lines up to merge with the existing seams just below the knee. Cut off excess seam allowance, pin, tack and machine.

Altering the fit of a dress or skirt at the waist involves unpicking the waistband or seam and increasing or decreasing the size of darts and seams evenly all round. The same technique can be used on trousers, but if the fabric is heavy – denim is particularly difficult – it's very hard to sew through the many thicknesses involved. A sharp new heavyweight sewing-machine needle helps.

Dyeing
Yellowing whites or faded plain colours can be revived by dyeing. Multi-purpose (hot water) dyes offer the best colour range and can be used on almost all fabrics, but you need a large heat-proof vessel to do the job. Cold water dyes can be used in a bucket or sink, and although good on cotton, linen and rayon come out pale on poly-cotton mixtures, silk and wool, and are not suitable for anything else. Fabrics based on polyester do not take dye well, but a limited range of special polyester dyes is now available.

Whatever type of dye you use it will come with full instructions. Follow them exactly, and take great care not to spill the tiniest drop of dye solution or you will revive one article at the cost of another. Patterned fabrics can be over-dyed to change the basic colour but the pattern will still be there. A boyfriend once asked me to dye a waistcoat in an unwearably loud red tartan, and was delighted when over-dyeing it in bottle green resulted in a very chic tartan in varying subdued shades of green.

If you want to dye a dark-coloured garment a lighter shade, strip the old dye out first with proprietary colour and stain remover (Dygon). Another handy product is a white 'dye' which restores whiteness to a wide range of fabrics.

3 TABLEWARE

I was first introduced to the revolutionary idea that table settings do not have to consist of matching china, matching cutlery and matching glasses when staying with a friend who fed a large family every day, plus endless visitors. Her kitchen dresser was piled high with plates, the shelves were crammed with cups and glasses and the drawers overflowed with cutlery. I never managed to find even two pieces alike, but once laid on the table everything seemed to blend together perfectly well. Moreover there were no ugly scenes when hasty young washers-up smashed a plate or two, and if cutlery got swept into the rubbish bin, as mine frequently does, nobody even noticed.

Everybody loves pretty china, so it's not easy to acquire nice pieces cheaply that are not chipped or cracked. (Such items are all right for display, but not for eating off.) But if you are always on the lookout, and pick up a bit here and a bit there, you can gradually build up a collection. Even the most commonplace china usually has the maker's name and symbol stamped underneath, and as pieces accumulate it is interesting to see what names keep turning up: some famous ones still in business, some long forgotten.

Because china is so popular it is ridiculously overpriced by some secondhand dealers; bear in mind that quite reasonable-looking modern earthenware dinner plates can be bought for around a pound. Porcelain, or bone china, naturally costs considerably more, and buying secondhand is a way of acquiring some cheaply. In charity shops or at jumble sales you can often find a bone china saucer or plate hiding among a stack of common earthenware; a quick way to tell one from t'other is to hold it up to the light and see if it is delicate enough for your fingers to show through. However, earthenware is in many ways preferable for daily use, as it is less liable to break. Hard-baked earthenware called stoneware or ironstone is even more indestructible.

Another way of getting your hands on secondhand china, and free, is from friends and relations who still believe in keeping up middle-class standards and buying matching sets. The remnants of their old ones are bound to be skulking in cupboards, too good to throw away but never used.

Should you insist on your china matching there are two ways to acquire it secondhand. Quick way: buy the fag-end of a Victorian dinner or tea service at an auction. As the Victorians had such large families, and entertained on a grand scale, the original services ran to hundreds of pieces, so what's left is ample for modern use. When buying a quantity of china always inspect every item, particularly plates at the bottom of the pile; the best ones will naturally all be on top. Remnants of more modern services can also be found, but as they were not so vast originally they may not contain sufficient for your needs. But designs from the great firms like Wedgwood, Royal Doulton, Royal Worcester and Johnson Brothers were often produced over very long periods of time, and you may well be able to buy new pieces to fill in the gaps in a service first put on the market over twenty years ago.

Slow way: build up a collection of any long discontinued mass-produced cheap line, say 1930s Woolworth's. Pieces do turn up fairly frequently, but it helps if you are able to travel around to different parts of the country.

The *in* china at the moment is anything vaguely art deco (see page 76). For this you will have to get up very early in the morning, to snatch it off market stalls in the grey dawn before dealers grab it for trendier markets or posh shops. You might be lucky if you've the time and patience to poke about in boxes of oddments gathering dust in some junk shop, but the trouble is that this china is usually clearly marked or even signed with the potter's name, and also once seen is instantly recognisable again. Names to look for include Clarice Cliff, Susie Cooper and Carlton Ware.

Glassware without chips and cracks is even more rare than china, so really old pieces are priced as collector's items, and too precious actually to use. But glasses of later date, particularly the more robust machine-pressed kind, are another matter. A lot of middle-aged to modern stuff is in quite appalling taste, crawling with moulding decorations, gilding and even inscriptions like 'Bottoms Up!' – fun to collect just to see how low it can sink. But cocktail glasses from the twenties and thirties in geometric shapes and often partly frosted are highly collectable, especially if accompanied by a matching cocktail shaker. Personally I do like to have glasses at least in sets of four, not for aesthetic reasons but because some dinner guests get edgy if their glass looks smaller than their neighbour's.

Decanters and water jugs, being more robust, are easier to come by, and the former can be pleasingly cheap if the stopper is missing, broken or jammed in place; or if the decanter itself is stained. Finding a replacement stopper is not impossible, if you can remember that you want one when browsing through oddment boxes, and the other faults can be rectified. Do not be fooled by antique-looking glass carafes stamped 1852. They turn up frequently in charity shops and are modern Californian wine bottles; nice but not worth more than 50p.

Boxes of cutlery oddments in junk shops and at jumble sales often contain nothing but rubbish, worn, bent and totally unappetising. Discard the worn-away chromium-plated stuff and look for stainless steel, or anything tarnished that might just be silver. It's not terribly likely, because any idiot can spot a hallmark – but you might get there before any idiot has looked. Acquiring cutlery by this method for more than one or two people is a slow process, so if you are serious you will be better off at auctions, jewellers dealing in secondhand silver, or pawnshops.

Just in case you don't already know: 'silver' is a loose term which can mean three quite different things. Most expensive is sterling silver, which is always hallmarked. If you intend to build up a collection of silver it is essential to get yourself a book and learn how to recognise the different hallmarks. Studying hallmarks has its own fascination; so much so that some collectors seem more interested in the hallmarks than the actual silver. Each item has four basic marks: the silversmith's own symbol or initials; the symbol of the assay office where it was tested, such as the London leopard's head; a date letter; and the assay mark of a lion passant indicating that the piece is of sterling quality (92.5 per cent silver).

Silver without these markings, often larger items like coasters and salvers, may be Sheffield plate: copper covered with a thin layer of silver. Sometimes the copper can be seen 'bleeding' through on sharp edges. Early Sheffield plate may have markings designed to pass it off as silver; some has none, and later stuff has the maker's name and symbol. All Sheffield plate is old as it stopped being made after 1840 when electro-plated nickel-silver was invented. The new invention is now generally known as silver plate, and every item is stamped EPNS. It is made by laying a thin coat of silver on to copper or nickel by electrolysis; the coating is extremely thin and eventually wears away in places.

A lot of silver and EPNS cutlery is made in classic designs such as fiddle pattern and king's pattern, which are endlessly repeated, so it is quite possible to build up reasonably matching settings. Old table knives may have plain carbon steel blades, which are a great nuisance as they discolour after contact with some foods, or it left wet, and can also smell nasty. But a carbon steel carving knife is well worth having, especially if there is a sharpening steel with it, as plain carbon steel sharpens up much better than stainless steel.

Stainless steel holloware – coffee and tea pots, jugs and so forth – is usually rather plain, not as much fun as the infinite variety of shapes, colours and patterns available in china, or as elegant as silver plate. But stainless steel keeps liquids hotter than anything else, which is one reason why it is so popular with hotels and restaurants, the other being that it does not require regular cleaning like silver. Both of these reasons may commend it to you too. Stainless steel is a comparatively modern invention. The first stainless steel tea service appeared at London's Ideal Home Exhibition in1934. As with so many other inventions it was not popular at first; of course in those days even quite modest households still had a domestic servant or two to clean the silver.

In your quest for tableware you will probably also come across quite a few kitchen items, some of which should be snapped up, others shunned. Large aluminium or tin fish kettles, and preserving pans, are expensive to buy new. Elaborate jelly moulds in china, copper and other materials are already collectables. Ordinary aluminium saucepans are usually far too dented and wobbly for use, especially if you have an electric stove, but one with a heavy ground or machined base could be a good buy. Enamel is suspect because the slightest chip renders it un-hygienic as the bare metal rusts; and some imported pans with orange enamel on the *inside* may be dangerous. Early non-stick coatings were not very durable and such pans are invariably wrecks by the time they reach the secondhand market. Copper pans come expensive, and if intended for use will probably need relining as well.

Other kitchen items that are fun to buy are the really old ones: Victorian coffee mills, mincing machines and marmalade cutters. You might even come across a knife-cleaning machine to clean those carbon steel knives.

RESTORATION WORK

Cleaning

China and glass Start with a good wash in hand-hot detergent solution, scrubbing any twiddly bits with a soft brush. A soaking in biological detergent will bring it up sparkling clean, but if any items have been glued together the joints may open up. To remove dirt from slight surface cracks or crazing soak the item in a washing-up bowl filled with cold water and a cup of household bleach; but watch out for very old and faded patterned china where the painting has been applied over the glaze – such a bath just might make it vanish altogether.

A strong solution of household bleach is also very good for removing heavy tannin stains from cups and inside teapots. But rinse thoroughly after using bleach or your next cup of tea will taste exceeding strange. A quicker method, effective on light staining, is to rub with bicarbonate of soda or borax on a damp cloth (they are both very mildly abrasive).

Old decanters often have nasty stains in the bottom. The time-honoured butler's method of cleaning them is to swill

round some kind of abrasive, variously given as anything from lead shot to egg shells, in a little liquid. Personally I find a soak in biological detergent more effective, plus the use of a bottle brush if necessary. (To release a stuck stopper either apply gentle heat – hot water or hot air from a hair-dryer – to the neck to cause the glass to expand; or tap the neck gingerly on the edge of a table.)

Old vases, whether of china or glass, may have a crusty lime deposit in the bottom. The recommended treatment is to fill the vase with either distilled water (as sold for steam irons) or rain water and leave for a week, after which the scale should be soft enough to scrub off. Again, you may need a bottle brush to reach it.

Cutlery and holloware Wash first, in your usual way, but scrub between the tines of forks to remove old food debris, and also pay attention to any ridges or ledges where dirt may have accumulated. Clean tarnished silver and silver plated items with Goddard's Silver Dip or Long Term Silver Polish. Do not use Silver Dip on stainless steel as it will spoil the finish; if such items are discoloured clean with Stainless Steel Care. Watch out with 'silver' knives: some have stainless steel blades, so should not be dipped.

Clean blackened carbon steel knife blades with household cleansing powder on a damp cork (this saves cutting your fingers); steel wool pads give a gleaming finish. Discoloured ivory handles may respond to rubbing with a lemon, which is a mild bleach. But do not try to bleach them white; they *should* be a soft yellowed colour.

To clean tannin-stained metal pots and spoons fill the pot with boiling water, add a teaspoon of denture cleaner plus any spoons and leave overnight. Altenatively use biological detergent; but not household bleach.

Pots and pans Removing burnt-on grease from aluminium pans is hard work but can be done very successfully. Start by using steel wool and scouring powder; finish with steel wool pads to give a high shine. To clean discoloured aluminium boil up some water in the pan containing chunks of squeezed lemons or stalks of rhubarb.

Copper needs gentler treatment. Use only a very fine

abrasive, such as coarse salt on the face of a cut lemon, to rub over the surface. Alternatively use a proprietary product designed for cleaning copper, such as Goddard's Glow.

Vitreous enamel is hard to clean as any harsh treatment is liable to scratch the surface. Rub very gently with scouring powder on a damp cloth; but never use steel wool. If discoloured fill with a 1:4 solution of bleach and water and leave overnight; rinse thoroughly.

Repair

China and glass To stick back jug and cup handles, rejoin broken lids and the stems of glasses use the techniques described on pages 77-8.

Cutlery To reunite detached knife blades with their handles first scrape out all the old gunge from inside the handle; a screwdriver will do the job well. Use this again to pack the handle about two-thirds full with epoxy resin adhesive (wipe screwdriver blade clean with nail varnish remover or methylated spirit). Push the tang of the knife blade in; wipe off any surplus resin. Bind round with sticky tape and leave overnight.

Ordinary steel knives can be sharpened on an oilstone or in a patent sharpener. Scalloped blades can be honed, but on the flat side only; saw-tooth knives cannot be sharpened. Flatten bent tips by hammering on an anvil or a flat piece of steel; straighten a buckled blade by fixing it between two blocks of wood in a vice and gently levering straight. Nicks can be removed with a slipstone or fine file.

Forks: lever bent tines apart by inserting a ruler in between them; or place the fork in a cloth in a vice and tighten the jaws.

Spoons: provided they are just household spoons, not silver, dents can be hammered out. If the dent bulges *into* the bowl place the spoon on a block of wood and gently hammer the bulge out with a ball pein (round-ended) hammer. Bulges the other way are more difficult to fix, as you have to make a cast to the shape of the spoon bowl, which will not shatter when you put the spoon on top of it and hammer. I wouldn't bother, myself.

Pots, pans and holloware Dents in thin metal can sometimes be successfully removed by the technique described on page 83.

But a heavy-gauge aluminium saucepan may prove too strong for this.

Saucepan handles are a much easier proposition. Very old pans often had a wooden handle fitted into a metal socket with a screw. If this is burnt or missing it is simple to make a replacement. More modern saucepans have handles fixed by three rivets. If they are loose get hold of two good-sized hammers and a helper. The helper holds the saucepan firmly on a table with one hammer under each rivet in turn; you strike the rivets firmly with the other. Some pans also have a long screw running right through the handle which may need tightening.

If a saucepan lid lacks its knob simply buy a screw-on plastic one from a hardware store. A broken or missing handle can easily be fixed if you have a pair of metal snips and a pop riveter. Cut a piece of metal from an empty tin, fold it lengthwise like bias binding so there are no sharp edges, hammer flat and rivet in place.

4 HOUSEHOLD EQUIPMENT

Buying secondhand household equipment, most of which runs on either electricity or gas, is fraught with hazard. If the thing works when you buy it, it may partly or totally give up the ghost by the time it has endured a bumpy ride home, or at any moment thereafter. And even if it works, is it safe?

Three authorities I approached on your behalf (The Electricity Council, British Gas Corporation and Trading Standards Office) would all really prefer it if no one bought secondhand equipment at all. This may be all very well in an ideal world, but in the real one old appliances are changing hands every day of the week. Many young couples setting up home for the first time just can't afford £200 for a new cooker, plus several hundred more for the multiplicity of equipment now deemed necessary to run the modern home. (I counted 15 electric motors in my house and garage, and the average household probably has more.) Also by no means all the appliances on the market are clapped out and dangerous. There are plenty of rich and/or silly people around who get rid of equipment for no better reason than that it is filthy, doesn't go for some trivial reason, or because they want the latest, flashiest model. Perfectly good household stuff also comes on to the market because people die or sell up home.

What follows is an attempt to arm you with enough knowledge to spot the lemons, buy the bargains, and use them safely.

Where you buy is just as important as what. The safest place of all is a Gas or Electricity Board showroom, as they cannot afford to sell anything even slightly substandard, and won't have shut up shop and decamped if you return a few weeks later with a complaint. Unfortunately they confine themselves to cookers, and supply is limited and erratic. But every one is reconditioned, tested and cleaned and carries a solid 6- or 12-month guarantee.

The next best place is a retailer who specialises in secondhand equipment, and has a reputation to live up to – as opposed to a junk dealer who handles anything and everything. There are still a few shops like this sprinkled around, usually in less smart areas of town; some do mainly white goods (cookers and refrigerators), others brown goods (TV sets, radios and stereo equipment). Such shops test, recondition and clean their goods, and should offer a limited guarantee in that they will carry out repairs if something goes wrong shortly after purchase.

Private sales often give the best opportunity to see an appliance connected up so it can be thoroughly tested; but this is the situation where your legal rights are lowest (see page 123).

When buying electrical equipment, in particular, anywhere else one must enter into the transaction in the spirit of having a flutter on a dubious nag, especially if there is no opportunity to test the goods. If a vacuum cleaner picked up at an auction for a fiver turns out dud, you lost the bet; but it might go like a bomb for years, and you won.

Wherever you buy consider the question of spare parts. If the amount of money involved is small you may take the view that the item is strictly expendable, and just hope it won't pack up before you consider you've had your money's worth. But with something more expensive, like a cooker, it's as well to get the maker's name and the serial number of the appliance, which should be on a rating plate, usually at the rear, to check up before buying to see if spare parts are still available, and also servicing. With electrical appliances check the colours of the wires in the flex. If they are the current blue/brown/green-yellow ones, the chances of getting spares are much higher than if they are the old red, black and green ones, as the appliance is that much younger. (Colours were changed in about 1963.) The maker's name is another guide. Reputable manufacturers should keep stocks of functional parts for 12-15 years for large appliances, 10 years for small ones. But if the brand name is obscure and/or foreign you can probably forget it. Spares for white goods made in America are unobtainable, as their makers pulled out of the British market, taking their spares with them, when cheap Italian goods started to pour in.

But the spare parts scene is not all gloom. New models are not constructed entirely of new parts, so often those available will still fit a golden oldie. I have an extremely vintage coal-effect electric fire of hideous aspect which saved me from freezing to death one extra-cold winter. I was prepared to write it off when first one bar, then another went, but was pleasantly surprised to get new ones over the counter; they didn't even have to be specially ordered. New radiant rings for old cookers are also available, provided they are well-known makes. And mechanical geniuses with plenty of garage space can keep the most obscure antediluvian equipment going by having a complete spare appliance stowed away from which to cannibalise parts.

Whatever you buy make sure it's safe. Working is not necessarily the same thing as working safely. So with electrical appliances check out all the points covered on page 66. If anything about it still gives cause for concern have it looked at by a competent electrician. Gas appliances should always be checked and installed by a trained gas fitter – see page 64.

Electrical equipment

Cookers Check that radiant rings, oven and grill elements and any spit-roasting mechanism are all working. If this cannot be done you should have an assurance from the seller that they do, plus a guarantee to pay for replacements if this proves not to be the case. Testing a thermostat involves putting a kitchen thermometer in the oven to see if the reading tallies with the chosen setting. Complicated bits like pre-setting devices will usually have to be taken on trust even if the cooker is still installed. Also check for filthy oven, chipped enamel, rust at the bottom of the cabinet, missing parts and ill-fitting oven doors.

Micro-wave cookers are potentially extremely dangerous if there should be any leakage of the electro-magnetic waves. If you do buy one secondhand make sure it has a BEAB or Electricity Council safety label, and have it serviced *before* you start using it.

Refrigerators Most refrigerators are the compression type. To test turn the temperature dial to high and listen. The motor should cut in immediately, and after a few minutes the condenser on the back should start to feel warm. Check the age of a refrigerator by the flex colour code method if nothing else is available; the estimated life of a compressor is 12 years, and they are expensive to replace. Also check that the door seal is OK; close it on a piece of paper, which should not then pull out.

Washing machines and spin-dryers Because of their moving parts these are extremely trouble-prone; even new ones are not totally reliable, so obviously elderly ones are even more likely to let you down. Also the fact that contact with water is involved makes them potentially more dangerous than most other equipment. They may also be rusty inside and stain the clothes. Probably not a good buy unless coming from someone you know, with a convincing reason for selling (like going broke or emigrating to Australia), who will let you try out the machine.

With spin-dryers, make sure that the lid cannot be opened before the machine stops or slows right down. This has only been mandatory since 1975.

Dishwashers Very similar cases to washing machines. And if you have old secondhand crockery and cutlery it may not like being machine washed anyway.

Heating appliances Bar fires and infra-red (bathroom) heaters are simple things and easy to repair. Only buy those with glass-enclosed elements, which are relatively modern. Do not buy if the reflector is irreparably tarnished, as heat will not be reflected outwards as it should be.

Convector and fan heaters are rather more complicated, and replacement elements for convectors may not be available. A convector with a thermostat is preferable to one without.

In oil-filled radiators the heating element is sealed away so you can't replace it. They do have thermostats, but on old ones the controls are less sophisticated than they are today, so they may still waste heat.

Night storage heaters are best avoided. Old ones were designed to work with an afternoon boost, which is not now available at cheap rate because modern heaters have sophisticated controls or are designed to work on the Economy 7 half-price tariff, which is nights only. They are also extremely heavy to transport, unless you are prepared to take them apart in which case you will need professional help in reassembling them.

Bear in mind that any type of electric heater can be a very expensive form of heating. Nevertheless they can be useful items to have in reserve as back-up heating or for emergency use – say if your central heating breaks down when there's a foot of snow outside the door.

Brown goods TV sets, transistor radios and stereo equipment are items of such mind-boggling complexity that buying one secondhand must always be a gamble. The economics of buying a secondhand colour TV are problematical, because on top of the purchase price you may need to pay an engineer to get it working satisfactorily, and bear the cost of repairs if anything goes wrong. But a secondhand set hired from a rental company does not cost much initially (you don't have to pay 6 months in advance); they pay for installation and also subsequent repairs. (I once had a colour TV set completely burnt out when the roof aerial was hit by lightning and was extremely glad I did not own it.) But if you're looking for a second set to scotch quarrels between addicts of Dallas and Brookside, or because the children commandeer the main one for horrible video games, a secondhand one might be the answer. Always buy from a shop specialising in reconditioned sets, where you will be able to get it repaired.

As radios are one of the few things that get cheaper as the years go by, and most people don't throw them out until they are worn-out, crackly wrecks, they are not often a good buy. If one in good condition comes your way check that it's not on the market because it doesn't get long-wave reception, and was discarded for that reason when Radio 4 moved to the long waveband in 1978.

Stereo equipment is even more of a minefield, and unless you know quite a bit about it you can be badly hit. But on the other hand it's a field where people often get rid of perfectly good stuff, either because they are moving on to greater things, or because they have a sudden need to raise some cash. As I know nothing whatsoever about this sort of thing I would only buy from a personal friend – and not all of those either – with advice from someone who does know a woofer from a tweeter.

Small appliances Many of these, such as hair-dryers and toasters, are deliberately made so that they cannot easily be repaired by DIY methods, if at all, so should never be bought unless you can test that they are working perfectly. Don't touch secondhand electric blankets; the risks involved if one is sub-standard or faulty are just too great.

Avoid appliances with cracked plastic casing. As well as being potentially dangerous, this may be an indication that they have been dropped hard at some time, which won't have improved their chances of a long and happy life.

Food mixers and liquidisers are items which get a lot of hard wear, and quite possibly misuse. Bent beaters can be put right easily, but only if spares are available. Once the motor goes the machine is a write-off; unless the problem is only worn carbon brushes which can be replaced. A machine is more valuable if it still has the instruction manual; and check carefully that it has all its accessories.

An electric slow-cooker or frying pan should always be tested before purchase as the commonest fault is a burnt-out element; this can only be done if it has an indicator light. Also check the food container and lid carefully for cracks, chips and burnt-on food, and do not buy unless replacements can be had. Feel a non-stick surface for signs that it has been damaged by harsh cleaning; if it feels rough it won't be non-stick any more.

Light fittings The main problem with old lamps is that many won't conform to the latest electrical safety regulations for light fittings, which require metal ones to be earthed – that is the flex must have three wires, not just two, unless they are double insulated. As it is not very easy for the amateur to establish whether a light fitting is safe or not, it's best to have them looked at by an electrician. This is essential with *very* old lamps, like the art deco types now so popular, if you bought them anywhere other than from a specialist lighting emporium where everything is guaranteed safely rewired.

Vacuum cleaners Testing before purchase is essential, not just to find out if it goes, but to make sure it has adequate suction. A good cleaner should lift up the corner of a loose-laid carpet or rug. Supplies of spare parts are pretty good, even for quite old cleaners, as they have changed very little since they were first introduced in the early 1900s (though I don't suggest you buy one *that* old!). Spares are often cheaper on market stalls than in shops. Other points to check before buying are squeaky wheels and worn beater brushes on upright models; splits in the flexible hose, worn brushes and missing attachments on cylinder models.

Water heaters These are not something I would buy myself. If you cannot see the appliance installed there is no way of telling if it works. And water combined with electricity is a dangerous, possibly lethal combination. If you do buy one always have it installed by a qualified electrician, and serviced as well if it is not guaranteed reconditioned.

Other equipment

Oil heaters Secondhand oil heaters can be extremely dangerous, because old models were not designed to the same high standards as modern ones, and have been the cause of many tragic fires. If you do buy one, get it from a specialist dealer. The Oil Heaters (Safety) Regulations 1977 make it an offence to sell a secondhand heater that does not conform to the same standards of safety as are imposed on manufacturers of new ones. In order to stay in business, the specialist is far more likely to comply with these regulations than a general dealer who sells the odd heater or two without anyone being any the wiser. However, prosecution is no compensation if your house burns down, so make sure it is established that the heater has been thoroughly overhauled.

After that it's up to you: many fires start because heaters are being improperly used. Keep them clean, with well-trimmed wicks, and don't stand them in a draught. Do not fill while lit, splash oil about, over-fill or carry when lit. Do not let the flame burn too high, or unevenly. Stand them in a hearth or at least against a wall, to reduce the danger of their being knocked over. If children are present, avoid radiant heaters (the ones with a mesh dome that glows) and screw convectors (the enclosed type) to wall or floor.

Personally I wouldn't use an oil heater unless it was the only alternative to frostbite. I have lived with them in the past, and they all give off gallons of water, making windows stream, and are often smelly. The convector ones are fairly trouble-free, but the radiant ones are temperamental brutes. In those days their saving grace was cheapness, but since the price of oil zoomed up ten years ago even that has been whittled away.

Sewing machines (hand, foot and electric) As modern sewing machines are both hideously complicated and horrendously expensive, an old one in working order is a good buy if you are a less-than-fanatical home sewer. Old ones are simple, sturdy creatures and rarely go wrong. But checking on the availability of spare parts is still advisable, as although their machines go marching on many of the manufacturers are no more. The Singer company is still going strong, though, and can supply spare parts, old instruction manuals and useful information on how older machines work.

The oldest and cheapest type of machines are the hand-operated ones. These probably do only one thing: straight stitch forward, but they are quite adequate if all you want to do is run up the occasional pair of curtains or a cushion cover or two. Their main drawback is that as one hand is used to turn the wheel, only one is free to guide the work; and of course they are slow.

The old treadle sewing machines are much faster, leave both hands free, and the foot-operated treadle mechanism is easy to use once you've practised a bit and got the hang of it. They are a useful piece of furniture, too – the machine folds under a small table top when not in use. They should give forward straight stitch and reverse, useful for finishing off a seam.

Early electric machines do no more than this, but much faster, and with no effort from you. Later ones offer more and more different stitches and other facilities. If you do dressmaking it's worth paying more for a machine that at least does a zig-zag stitch, as this is so useful for finishing seams neatly and quickly – it stops the cut edges fraying.

Always try using a machine before you buy, not only to see if it works, but to find out, in the absence of an instruction manual, whether you can operate it. Test all the available stitches, in both forward and reverse. A different-coloured thread top and bottom helps you to see if the stitches are lying properly in the fabric, not too loose and not too tight. If the machine puckers the material up, breaks the thread or produces loops in the under-stitching, try adjusting the tension, but if that doesn't do the trick reject it.

Beware of advertisements for secondhand machines in newspaper small ads. Most of these are placed by unscrupulous dealers who tempt the reader with an incredibly cheap secondhand model, but turn up on the doorstep and do a hard sell for a new machine.

Gas equipment

Now that only natural gas is piped to UK households, the danger of being poisoned by a gas escape has gone, and you cannot commit suicide with it should you feel so inclined. (But you can still be made very ill or even killed by carbon monoxide poisoning. This can happen with any fuel if the flue is blocked and the fumes flow back into the room instead of being vented to the outside.) Escaping gas is still dangerous if there is a considerable build-up in a room, as it can cause a mighty explosion which could blow your house up. You should also know that such an explosion might be considered your fault, and you could be fined up to £400. All of which could turn a secondhand buy into a very bad bargain indeed.

In general British Gas advise against buying secondhand gas appliances; but many people do. So if you join them always observe these four rules:

1 Buy from a reputable source, as outlined at the beginning of this chapter.
2 Have the appliance installed either by the Gas Board, or by a registered Corgi installer. He is not a supplier of royal dogs, but a member of the Confederation for the Registration of Gas Installers, and guaranteed competent.
3 Locate the mains supply tap so that you can turn it off promptly if noticing any suspicious gassy smell. (The tap will be near the meter, and is off when the notched line on the spindle points *across* the pipe.) Then open windows and contact the Gas Board.
4 Have appliances serviced every year to make sure they continue to operate safely and economically.

Another point to bear in mind when buying secondhand gas equipment is that the changeover to natural gas ten years ago meant that all appliances then in use had to be converted in order to burn it. Theoretically you should not be able to buy an unconverted appliance, which would be extremely dangerous. But although safe, some converted appliances never worked quite as well afterwards. Some cooker burners, for instance, could not be turned down as low as before. So unless the seller can assure you that the appliance is a post-conversion model, check with the manufacturers before buying.

Cookers Check these out as for electric cookers, page 58. In addition, check that there is a working ignition system. If not it is worth less money as you will have to buy a gas lighter and have the inconvenience of using it.

Fires Modern gas fires supply both radiant heat and convected heat – via the grille on the top. So they are far superior to the old type which only provided heat from the radiants. They also have a choice of heat settings. If the radiants are broken check before buying that replacements can be bought. Most of these fires have to be fitted into an existing hearth so that waste gases go up the chimney, unless they are the balanced flue type which can be fitted against suitable outside walls. Gas wall heaters also need balanced flue installation.

Freestanding gas fires which burn gas from a cylinder and do not need a flue are popular secondhand buys, safe if bought from a reputable shop and used with due care. But they are a poor form of heating as they give off a lot of moisture and may cause or add to condensation problems.

Built-in cooking appliances (hobs, ovens and grills or spit-roasters). As these are all relatively new inventions, bought by the better-off, they should be a good buy if the price is right.

Water heaters Instantaneous water heaters are economical as they only heat the water when the tap is turned on. They can be single-point, for kitchen sinks; or multi-point to serve a bath, washbasin and maybe sink as well. New water heaters are all of the balanced flue type, which is very safe because the waste gases are sealed away from the room and discharged directly to the outside. When older models are used observe the following safety precautions: open the door or window while running the hot water, turn the heater off before getting into the bath and do not then relight it. Make sure the bathroom has a permanent ventilator which is unblocked. Small sink heaters with no flue should not be run for more than 5 minutes at a time.

RESTORATION WORK

Most of the equipment covered in this chapter is electrical, which makes repair work fairly minimal. With really vintage stuff you won't be able to get spare parts; modern items are often specially designed to seal away any possibility of repair – the whole idea is for you to buy a new one. But nonetheless quite a lot can be done. Anything not mentioned here is either absent because I have already recommended you not to buy it secondhand in the first place (electric blankets) or because home repair is *out* (TV sets and gas appliances).

Electrical safety

Whatever you buy, if it has a plug fitted check this out straight away. If it is cracked or broken, has worn pins or a missing cord grip replace it at once – *not next week*. Even if it looks OK open it up: do not rely on the previous owner to have wired it up correctly. The wires (brown or red to the live terminal; blue or black to neutral; green or green/yellow stripes to earth) should be neatly and securely fixed, with no bare metal showing. The cord grip should be firmly screwed down above the point where the outer plastic casing has been stripped off. Also check that the fuse is right. Most equipment needs the 13amp fuse already fitted in a new plug, but low-power items like light fittings, radios, record players and small hand-held appliances should have a 3amp fuse.

A standard-size electric cooker cannot just be plugged into an ordinary electric socket. A cooker control unit is required, which has a higher rating to cope with the load when all or most of the burners are used at the same time. Mini cookers and other small electric cooking appliances can be used in an ordinary socket; if in any doubt read the plate on the back to check that the wattage rating is no more than 3kW.

Also check out the flex for fraying, splits, cracking or burns in the outer cover. Replace if you find any; all are potentially dangerous. Irons and kettles are specially prone to frayed flex.

Bearing in mind that electricity is a killing force, don't tackle any repair or inspection without observing basic safety rules:

1 Unplug the appliance from the power supply *first*.
2 When fitting a new part, such as a cooker element, make quite sure to wire it up in exactly the same way as the old one; make a colour drawing if it looks at all complicated.
3 If any doubts or difficulties arise swallow your pride and hand over to an electrician; don't take chances.

If the flex on an appliance is not long enough, do not join a bit on, even with a connector, and certainly not with a bit of insulating tape. Either replace it, or use the appliance with a proper extension lead.

Electrical equipment is mainly fixed together with Phillips and Pozidriv screws, so you'll need matching screwdrivers in appropriate sizes to get inside things.

Cookers If your bargain cooker is caked with grease and the oven has a thick dark brown coating that looks like stove enamel but is not, you have a Herculean task ahead. Buy the most powerful oven cleaner you can find and leave it on overnight, whatever the instructions may say about how it works wonders in an hour or two. (Don't apply these cleaners to aluminium parts.) Remove it as instructed. Remove any really stubborn burnt-on bits with a sharp razor blade in a holder; used gently it should not scratch the enamel, but even if it does what have you got to lose? Use steel wool pads on shiny metal bits, but never on enamel. Unclog blocked jets on gas rings with a piece of thick wire (don't use match sticks – they break off and get irretrievably stuck in).

Chipped enamel can be repaired with a special heat-proof paint sold at hardware stores; it's easy to use as it has a brush inside the bottle, like nail varnish. Do not try to refurbish a dingy-looking cooker with ordinary gloss paint; it won't stand up to the heat and constant cleaning.

If the hot-plates work but the oven doesn't, check that this is not merely because the timer is set in such a way as to prevent it. Failed lights in ovens or over hobs probably just need new bulbs; a fluorescent hob light might need a new starter.

When a hot-plate works but appears defective in any way replace it. Left alone it could eventually short circuit and blow a hole in what's bound to be your best saucepan, as well as blowing the cooker fuse. All hot-plate elements can be replaced, providing you can get the part, and it is a simple job, especially on some older cookers with solid plates (as opposed to spiral rings) which just plug in. Quote the model number of the cooker to your Electricity Board showroom or electrical retailer and they may be able to supply a new element from stock; sometimes they have to be ordered from the manufacturers. Grill and oven elements are a job for the service engineer.

Fires Elements for modern electric bar fires are enclosed in glass tubes, and replacements should be readily available. You may also be able to find the older ones where the wire coils round a fireclay cylinder. Handle them all carefully, as they are

fragile, and wire them up in exactly the same way as the old ones. While the element is out of the way give the reflector a good polish with impregnated wadding (do not use an abrasive metal polish) – a dull reflector reduces heat output.

Irons A secondhand iron is almost bound to have a flex that's fraying where it catches on the edge of the ironing board, and this should be replaced as it's potentially dangerous since exposed wiring could come into contact with damp washing or a wet pressing cloth. Replacing it is a fiddly job, as in the common sort of iron the ends of the flex are tightly jammed into a very small area under the pilot light cover. But some superior types have a removable flex coupler, like an electric kettle. Make sure the replacement flex is the right type, designed for use with irons. Other jobs you can do are replace a dead pilot light bulb; fit a new temperature control knob if the old one is broken; and shine up the sole plate – use special cleaner or a *very* mild abrasive, not household scouring powder.

Kettles As with irons replace fraying flex. If the kettle packs up, before rushing out for a new element check for loose wires in the plug, and misalignment of the contacts on the kettle itself (inside the plastic shroud). If that doesn't do the trick unplug, unscrew the shroud and ease the element out. Take it to an electrical shop and find out whether replacements are available. A new element will have two washers with it; there should also be instructions, but if not: the rubber washer goes on the element, *inside* the kettle, and the fibre one on the *outside*, under the shroud. (Note: automatic kettles, the sort that switch themselves off when the water boils, need professional attention.)

Some geriatric kettles have a primitive type of safety cut-out, a spring-loaded rod which pops out and ejects the flex coupler if it boils dry. This has to be reset manually by pushing it back in with, say, the end of a wooden spoon. Kettles with no safety cut-outs should not be bought.

Refrigerators If scratched and dowdy, a refrigerator can be rejuvenated with a coat of paint; an aerosol spray will give the best finish. But first make sure it is absolutely clean and grease-free, and sand lightly with wet-or-dry abrasive paper to give the new paint a grip.

If the refrigerator is noisy check that it is standing absolutely level. Possible repairs are few: fitting a new light bulb inside, and replacing the door seal if it unscrews, but not if it is clipped into a recess.

Spin-dryers Quite a few repairs can be done to these if you are mechanically minded. If the motor runs but the drum fails to spin, the belt drive can be adjusted or a new one fitted. A new gasket can be fitted to a leaking pump. The brake cable which slows the drum when the motor is switched off can be tightened or slackened, provided it is accessible, or a new one fitted.

Toasters Amateur repairs are not recommended for these, but the trouble may be no more than innards full of old crumbs. Unplug, turn upside down and remove the crumb tray. Shake out crumbs and wipe tray clean.

Vacuum cleaners If a cleaner operates feebly or not at all first check that the dust bag is not chock full. Also check for loose wires in the plug and where the flex enters the cleaner body. Clean or replace the felt filter pad on spherical models. On these and cylinder models check pipes and hose for blockages by pushing a long looped-over piece of strong wire (unwound coat hanger) gently through. Also check hoses for splits; bind up with strong sticky tape (insulating or carpet tape). On upright models unplug, remove the cover plate and check for string round motor blades, also worn brush rollers or drive belt. These can easily be replaced provided you can get spares.

Washing machines Very little can be done to these by the amateur. To keep a trusty old warhorse galloping be sure to clean the filter dish or plug after every use, and pat the machine dry inside with an absorbent cloth to keep rust at bay. Damaged hose can be repaired by inserting a piece of copper tube that fits tightly inside. Cut out the damaged section with a hacksaw and secure the tube at each end with a jubilee clip.

Electric motors Appliances powered by an electric motor are often a complete write-off once the motor packs up. But if it is a brush motor, as opposed to an induction motor, failure may simply be due to worn brushes. Rescue may be possible *if* you can get at the motor in the first place, and *if* replacement brushes are available; they must be exactly the same type.

Recognise a brush motor by its shape: it is longer than it is wide (an induction motor is more compact). Also look for the two brushes – all that will be visible from outside the casing are the two screws or clips, exactly opposite one another, which fix the brushes in place. A 'brush' is not a brush at all but a piece of graphite on the end of a spring. There is one on each side of the commutator, the segmented copper drum from which the drive shaft protrudes. As the commutator turns the brushes wear away at the ends in contact with it, and may eventually crumble altogether. Repair is simply a matter of unscrewing or unclipping each brush and replacing it with a new one.

5 PURELY ORNAMENTAL

Plenty of people collect secondhand bric-a-brac with which to decorate their homes. Indeed with some it becomes such a mania that they can hardly move for china figurines, oil lamps, seaside souvenirs, flat irons, enamelled advertisement plaques for long-gone brands of tea, stuffed parrots, Tiffany lamp-shades, plaster ducks and art deco clocks. All these things have their charms, but they can be quite pricey, because they are *in* (in certain circles!) and dealers know that. What gives me the greatest pleasure is finding objects which at first sight appear to be useless rubbish. The kind of things I have in mind should be mostly dirt cheap, or better still free. Often they need a bit of doing up, which again recommends them to me. It's a lot more fun to restore a pathetic, neglected artefact to its original state than just buy an object and stick it straight on a shelf. And many of them allow you to give free rein to your imagination; you can go beyond simple restoration and do something outrageously unsuitable just for the hell of it – like painting a formerly sedate object in pink and white stripes.

Empty bottles are among my favourite decorative objects. While my collection includes a few of the sought-after ones which are no longer cheap, most are modern wine and spirit bottles of pleasing shape which cost nothing. Good hunting grounds for exotic empty bottles are at the back of posh restaurants – I have a marvellous dark green, heavily ribbed champagne bottle which I picked up at Rules in London – and around full-up bottle banks in up-market areas where Spanish plonk is not the only tipple. On the whole I prefer green glass bottles left plain, but sometimes I paint designs on them, either directly on the glass, or on a coloured background. I use a Chinagraph pencil to outline the design, and paint with tinlets of gloss; spray cans are good for background coats. Painting bottles black inside gives them a mysterious medieval look. Don't attempt to do this with a paint brush – just pour a little paint in and swirl it around, then pour off the surplus. I have only managed to make this work with the pot-bellied Mateus wine bottles; with other shapes not enough air gets inside to dry the paint.

To acquire some of the now highly collectable antique bottles, like the cobalt blue ribbed ones once containing poisons, and ginger beer bottles with glass marble stoppers, try digging rather than shopping. Research is required, for most of these are excavated from Victorian rubbish dumps, along with other interesting finds like china potlids. But you might be lucky digging in your own back garden. As regular refuse collection is comparatively recent, many long-settled neighbourhoods have all sorts of rubbish buried in odd corners. In Kent, where the Romans first settled, it is still possible to dig up Roman coins complete with emperor's head. (Once I

thought I had found one, but scraped clean it proved to be an Ovaltinie badge, *circa* 1930, minus pin. But I did find a seventeenth – century goat bell.)

Most of what you dig up is broken and useless, though interesting. Everywhere I have gardened I've come across remnants of the cheap clay pipes that old men were still smoking in the late thirties (price a halfpenny in any pub), decanter stoppers and bits of old batteries. But I have also found several collectable bottles, including a cobalt blue one, a tiny white china bulldog in perfect condition, a miniature brown stoneware jar, several glass ink wells and dozens of marbles lost by children down the decades.

The great outdoors is also the place to find free if not exactly secondhand ornaments in the shape of natural objects. Shells, for instance. British shores do not yield any very large exotic ones; the most glamorous is the ormer, the one with a mother-of-pearl inside and an intriguing line of holes along one edge, and even that belongs in the Channel Islands. But any sandy beach may yield thousands of different small shells – winkles, cowries, painted tops, tellins; what turns up depends on where you are. (Also look for large sea urchin skeletons – they can get to the size of a human hand, but are usually much smaller.) In quantity small shells can be very ornamental, either stored in glass jars, drilled and made into necklaces, or used to decorate boxes and bottles in the manner beloved of Victorian ladies. The best time to search for shells is at low spring tide, which occurs for a few days every fortnight when the moon is either full or new.

While playing beachcomber also look for rocks and drift-wood scoured into interesting shapes by the sea. I have a paper-weight found at Whitstable which must once have been a red brick, but is now the size of a baked potato and perfectly smooth. Usually, though, natural rock is more interesting, as the wave action reveals intricate grain patterns. Personally I prefer sea-sculptured pebbles left alone, or just varnished to give them a shiny, wet look, and not painted to look like owls or pussycats; but it's a very popular pastime. Most people use poster paint for this, protected with poster varnish.

Cliffs by the sea are good places to look for fossils, interesting lumps of rock and also jet, the black hard stone once popular for making jewellery.

Another category of decorative items that you may be able to pick up here and there for nothing is the ancient key, the larger and more ornate the better. These don't look much singly, but once you start to build up a collection they can be attractively displayed. Some look best left alone, some can be polished up, others sprayed with black or metallic paint. I once bought a house from a man who had a collection of 600 keys, displayed on both sides of a massive hardwood beam supporting the upper storey. They looked splendid but caused no end of trouble once taken down, as the peppering of nail holes left behind caused my surveyor to think that the beam was infested with woodworm.

Now for things that you will have to pay *something* for, unless you have generous elderly relatives with well-stocked attics.

Pictures play a vital part in decorating a room, and it's a great thing that nowadays everyone can have a Rembrandt, a Gainsborough, a Degas or a Picasso by buying a colour print. These are very cheap for what they are, but if you then have to add on the cost of a new frame, it starts to add up. So – back to the junk shops and the auction rooms, which have plentiful supplies of truly terrible pictures, often displayed by the proud owner or perpetrator in magnificent frames. Dealers can be a bit obstinate about frames containing oil paintings and steel engravings, insisting on pricing them as works of art, however much you counter-insist that no one is ever going to come in and offer more than a price for the frame. Job lots bought at auctions can be a much better buy, going so cheap that even if you have to throw some of them away the purchase is still worth while. You should also be able to find empty frames, lacking not only picture but backing board and glass, and perhaps slightly damaged. Don't let this deter you: see page 80 for how to repair them. Hopelessly spotted old mirrors can also be bought for their frames.

Clocks were always considered decorative as well as useful, and had pride of place in the centre of the mantelshelf. A large one in working order, or a brass carriage clock, is not to be found cheap, but a smaller clock, whose mechanism long ago ticked its last tock, and perhaps has lost a hand or two, is a different matter. (And it's perfectly possible to make them go – see page 80). Many of these clocks have rather dark and dingy cases, and for them I make an exception to my usual rule of not over-painting hardwood, and decorate them in bright contrasting colours, picking out mouldings and twiddly bits in gold or black.

Brass and copper items are so popular that bargains are hard to come by, although you may find some so corroded and blackened that no one else fancies their chances at cleaning them up. The shiny copper warming pans and kettles, brass bells and trivets hanging all over low-class antique shops are invariably modern. No reason why you shouldn't buy them though – the metal looks the same unless you are an expert, and if the workmanship is of poorer quality at least the thing is not covered in dents. Horse brasses too, if priced at 50p or so, will be modern; but still nice, I think: so powerfully evocative of patiently-plodding plough horses and the countryside.

Which brings me to the whole question of fakes. As it is well known that the demand for particular kinds of antique decorative objects is far greater than the supply, copies are being turned out every day from factories in places as far apart as Spain and China. Of course, if you are following my advice and only buying things because you like them, and personally think the asking price not too exorbitant, this does not matter in the least. Often there is very little difference between the originals and the modern copies, at least to non-experts like you and me. Nevertheless, one does not like to be had . . .

All you can do is always suspect that something highly

desirable and not too expensive is a copy, and if this matters to you, familiarise yourself with the real things by studying them in museums, especially the Victoria and Albert in London. Also bear in mind that fakes are less likely to turn up at an auction of household effects than on a market stall. Items notorious for being widely copied include Staffordshire pottery figures, potlids, oil lamps, seamen's trunks, pewter ware, door porters and Mary Gregory glass, as well as brass and copper items of every description.

In recent years anything in the art nouveau or art deco styles has become so popular that no doubt it won't be long before these too start being faked. What exactly do these terms mean? Art nouveau is the older, and if you want to fix it in your mind go to a print gallery and look for the works of Alphonse Mucha: all curving female forms and intertwining leaves and flowers, not a straight line in sight. Mucha was a Czech, but the style originated in Britain, with the work of William Morris and the Arts and Crafts movement, and then swept the art world from about 1890 to 1910. It was applied to all the decorative arts: interior design (Mackintosh and Horta); glass work (Louis Tiffany) and book illustration (Aubrey Beardsley); and was taken up enthusiastically by potters, wood carvers, silversmiths, jewellery and textile designers.

Art nouveau designs are tranquil; art deco ones are lively, not to say frenzied. Art deco represents the jazz age, the machine age, the cinema and the cocktail bar. The name came from an exhibition of decorative arts and modern industries held in Paris in 1925. The style is full of geometric patterns and zigzags – sun rays were very popular themes, appearing on every radio, and still surviving on tins of Brasso – but some art deco pottery has floral designs such as foxgloves. Art deco was even more widely applied than art nouveau: Busby Berkeley choreography; Erté clothes; Clarice Cliff ceramics; Lalique jewellery; Odeon cinemas. The demand for art deco light fittings has grown so great that in 1983 the British Home Stores chain included two in their range, which are very characteristic: a naked lady holding up a globe-shaped lamp, and a pair of hands ditto.

In between the apparent junk and the highly sought after trendy items, nosing around junk shops and market stalls will reveal all sorts of decorative bits and pieces. Look for any china and glass whose shape, pattern or colour appeal to *you*, never mind the alleged origins; treen (anything made in wood and designed for use, from wooden spoons to objects so abstruse that not even the experts know what they are); old tins (some of these are already collectable; perhaps it's time to start a beer can vogue); old carpenter's tools, preferably in ebony with brass fittings – also collectables, but still likely to turn up here and there; nicely shaped wicker baskets; curious relics of the British Empire, like Benares brass ware, kukris and copper gongs, carved gourds and figures from Africa; anything made of beautiful natural materials like ivory, tortoiseshell, onyx or marble; scent bottles and costume jewellery (made of base metals and non- or semi-precious stones).

Seek, and ye shall find. . . . But don't expect bargains in well-known places like London's Portobello Road or The Lanes in Brighton. Backwaters are the places to fish.

RESTORATION WORK

China

With modern epoxy resin adhesives it is possible to make strong, near-invisible repairs to china. So as well as repairing pieces you have carelessly dropped you can undo old repairs made with thick brown glue or ugly rivets and remake them.

Old glue will generally give way if the item is soaked in hot water and detergent. If the pieces fail to separate, gradually make the water hotter and hotter; even boiling. If this fails try acetone (nail varnish remover). This is also good for removing any remaining traces of old glue – the break must be absolutely clean or new adhesive will not grip. If rivets are present pry them loose with a knife blade and extract with pliers. If they leave green stains behind dab with ammonia. Finally scrub the broken edges with detergent solution, rinse and dry. After that be careful not to finger the cut edges.

Warm the item in a low oven, apply epoxy resin to one surface (both if edges are large and porous), fit together and leave overnight in a warm room to harden. Use the adhesive sparingly so that it does not squeeze out; remove any that does while still soft with acetone, or when hardened with a razor blade. Something must be done to hold the broken pieces together while the glue cures. With plates, place pieces of gummed paper tape dipped in water across the break at frequent intervals, on both sides – the wet paper quickly dries out, shrinks and acts as a clamp. Jugs and cups can be supported in a container of sand, or a mound of Plasticine.

If a piece has multiple breaks mend it in stages; do not try to get all the pieces together in one go.

To repair a chip use a mixture of kaolin powder (from chemist's) and epoxy resin adhesive. Patience is required: spread the filler on thinly and build up several layers, leaving each one to dry between times. Build it up slightly above the original surface, then smooth down with a craft knife and wet-or-dry abrasive paper. Deep cracks can be treated in the same way, after thorough cleaning. (Soak the item in a bowl of cold water containing a cup of household bleach, but watch it just in case the pattern starts to fade.)

Colour the repair with enamel paint – use the tinlets sold in model and craft shops and mix colours together to get just the right shades. (These paints are guaranteed lead-free and non-toxic, so are all right if the item is to be used for food or drink.) If you get heavily into china repair a DIY kit is worth buying; this contains fillers, paints, brushes and glazes.

Glass

The technique for repairing glass is exactly the same as for china, but being transparent a join made with epoxy resin will be visible. An almost invisible repair can be made with one of the new wonder glues, but is not as strong. Follow the instructions very carefully; it is no exaggeration that these glues can stick your fingers together. I've done it and it's a frightening experience!

Picture frames and mirrors

Cleaning and repairing picture frames made of wood involves the same basic techniques as outlined for furniture, see page 20. Ornate frames, often gilded, are made by gluing plaster mouldings on to a wooden base, and these are often badly chipped or have chunks missing. Small areas can be built up with cellulose filler or plastic wood, then repainted or gilded. Do not use gold paint, which gives a cheap and nasty look, but wax gilt, sold in art shops. When whole sections are missing it will be necessary to take an impression from an undamaged piece and make a cast from it. This calls for dental impression compound (from dental suppliers), and the glass-fibre filler paste sold for mending holes in car bodywork. Stick the new section to the base with epoxy resin adhesive and seal with plaster primer (from art shops) before painting or gilding.

Theoretically a frame can be cut down to fit a smaller-sized picture (but it's the kind of job that can lead to tears and a frame only big enough to surround a postage stamp). Dismantle two diagonally opposed corner joints, mark the required size on the inside of the groove into which the picture will fit and cut with a tenon saw in a mitre box. The wider the picture frame moulding the more any inaccuracies in your mitre cutting will show, so practise on a narrow one first.

If the backing board is missing, or split, cut a new one from standard hardboard. I don't bother with glass for ordinary prints as the reflection inhibits one's view of them. For anything precious, and for original water colours, drawings or pastels, buy non-reflective glass – not cheap, but a great improvement.

Dark patches or spots on an old mirror show that the silver backing is peeling away. Resilvering is a professional job, and expensive. Buying new mirror glass would probably be cheaper, provided you settled for a flat sheet – most old mirrors have a bevel cut round the edge.

Pictures

Usually the pictures in old frames are hideous beyond belief, but if you happen on an old oil painting that you like, and assuming it's not a Rembrandt, you can magically improve it by a good clean. First remove the painting from its frame and place on a table, supported underneath so that no strain is put on the canvas while you work. Just wipe it over gently and evenly with a cotton-wool swab soaked in white spirit. *Never* use water. If it then looks flat and dull revarnish with modern synthetic picture varnish, using a large, new (dust-free) brush.

Even more sensational results can be obtained by removing old varnish which has turned brown, sometimes almost completely obscuring the picture. This is really a job for a professional, but as long as your find is strictly a no-value painting there's no harm in having a go. Set the picture up as for cleaning and have ready a saucer of acetone (the solvent – from chemist's), another of white spirit (solvent killer) and plenty of cotton wool. Start tentatively swabbing with the acetone at one edge to see what happens. It should dissolve the varnish; at any sign of colour on the swab, indicating dissolved paint, change to white spirit immediately to kill the action. Leave the painting to dry before revarnishing.

Watercolours and pastels need professional cleaning, but dirty prints can be cleaned up by rubbing them over lightly with lumps of fresh bread, plus discreet use of an artist's putty rubber. To remove grease stains from a paper picture dab it lightly with acetone, then cover with blotting paper and press briefly with a warm iron.

The brown spots known as foxing, caused by damp, can be removed from prints by light bleaching, provided they are not too large and numerous. Prepare a mixture of equal parts methylated spirit and hydrogen peroxide and apply to each spot with a fine artist's paint brush, watching closely. As soon as it begins to fade blot both sides of the print with blotting paper.

Clocks

Having bought a non-ticking clock for its decorative value alone why not try to get it going – if your efforts fail you can replace the original mechanism with a matchbox-sixed battery-operated modern one, which is what a clock mender, if you were able to track down one of this fast-vanishing breed, would probably do anyway. First give it a good clean: remove rust by rubbing parts with fine steel wool dipped in rust remover. Clean the movement by immersing it in lighter fluid or petrol for 15 minutes, then dry it with a hair-dryer. Oil with light machine oil, applying drops wherever moving parts touch, turning the hand control knob to distribute it. Missing hands, keys, even a new face, may be obtainable from a specialist supplier (see Yellow Pages under Clock and watch spare parts; also Useful Addresses, page 126). Large keys can also be improvised from copper tubing, if you fancy doing a bit of metal work. Take a square-section nail (the sort used to fix floorboards) and file it down to fit the winding shaft, then hammer a piece of copper tube over it to take on the shape; remove the nail. Cut a slot in the other end and insert another piece of tube, hammered flat, to make a handle. Join with epoxy resin adhesive.

Metal objects
Old metal, like hardwood furniture, develops a patina over the years which gives it unique character and charm, and this should be lovingly preserved. So even if items are heavily encrusted with grime, tarnish, corrosion or verdigris, start with gentle cleaning methods and only resort to drastic measures if absolutely necessary. Once your treasure is clean and shining you may be tempted to think of lacquering it so that it stays that way, but try to resist the temptation. Silver, in particular, never looks the same after lacquering. Also, as soon as an item gets the slightest scratch, the way is open for tarnish to develop underneath it, and the result looks even worse than all-over tarnish. Then there is the problem of what to do when the lacquer starts to break down and peel off; somehow it must all be removed.

However, if you are not over-keen on polishing, copper and brass items hanging up on a wall, or otherwise displayed and not used, will benefit from a coat of lacquer to keep them shining. Use transparent metal lacquer, not polyurethane varnish. There is no particular point in lacquering pewter or bronze, as it does not get dull all that quickly, and is not meant to have that sort of shine.

Gold, silver and silver plate Gold rarely tarnishes, but dirt and grease quickly detract from its appearance. To clean gold (and silver) jewellery simply immerse it in a jar of jewellery cleaning fluid.

Large, heavily tarnished silver pieces may be cleaned by first wiping them over with a cloth soaked in Silver Dip; if they still look yellowish, rinse and repeat. Then polish with Long Term silver polish, which leaves a protective barrier on the surface. This should be sufficient for medium tarnish on its own; for intricately chased or filigree pieces use Silver Foam which will reach into all the nooks and crannies.

Brass and copper Cleaning methods for these metals are broadly similar as they are closely related, brass being an alloy of copper and zinc. To clean items so badly neglected that they are black or green in colour, fill a large container or the sink with boiling water, add a cupful of washing soda and soak overnight. Any corrosion remaining after this may be removed with a burnishing brush, which has very fine brass bristles which will not scratch. For smaller items use the old-fashioned but very effective treatment of rubbing with a cut lemon dipped in coarse salt.

Less badly neglected items can be polished up with Goddard's Glow, a heavy-duty copper polish in a tube. Once back in tip-top condition keep them all shining with any proprietary metal polish recommended for brass and copper. (But do not polish items that are going to be lacquered.)

Pewter and Britannia metal These grey-coloured metals look very similar, and can be treated in the same way (old pewter is an alloy of tin and lead; Britannia metal and modern pewter are tin, antimony and copper). A really old piece is bound to be corroded. It can be bathed in washing soda solution, as above, but as this removes the patina which is a highly desirable characteristic of these metals, it is usually better to accept a degree of corrosion staining as a sign of genuine age. Normally, cleaning with brass and copper polish, which is slightly abrasive, will do the trick. Pewter which is really old, or pretending to be, is not supposed to have a high shine anyway, just a gentle glow. Long Term silver polish and foam can be used effectively on both metals, and are especially good on Britannia metal, which should have a silvery shine.

Bronze The greeny-blue patina is the distinguishing mark of old bronze, and if in good condition it should be left alone. Dust lightly to avoid rubbing abrasive particles into the metal and scratching it; do not polish or wash. Bright green spots are not patina, but bronze disease, caused by a damp atmosphere. Provided the item is not highly valuable brush these off with a burnishing brush, and if absolutely necessary scrape carefully with a knife. Bronze is an alloy of copper and tin.

Iron, steel and lead See pages 103-5.

Repairs Old copper kettles, pewter tankards and brass coal scuttles are inevitably somewhat dented. Some people like to keep the dents as signs that the article is genuinely aged, and not made in Birmingham last week. Dents naturally harbour dirt, so thorough cleaning will make them less noticeable. If you want to get rid of some really bad ones, the technique is to shape a piece of wood to match the curve of the kettle or whatever, put the dented part over this and press, smooth or hammer outwards until it has gone. (Be very careful with pewter as it is extremely soft.) This works in skilled hands; in mine it produces fresh dents.

Repairing fractures in brass, copper, bronze and pewter can be done by soft soldering, for which you need a soldering iron. Some joining may be possible using epoxy resin adhesive, as it will bond metal to metal and is very strong.

Ivory, tortoiseshell, bone and horn

As these are all of animal origin, items made from them should not be cleaned with water, as they may absorb it and swell. Wipe grease and dirt away gently with a cloth dipped in methylated spirit, using a soft brush to get into crevices. Polishing can be done with a very fine abrasive, such as metal polish, finishing off with silicone furniture polish.

Splits and cracks in ivory and bone can be restored with melted candlewax, but remember to keep the item away from heat afterwards. For breaks in any of these try epoxy resin adhesive.

6 TRANSFORMATION SCENES

The really advanced secondhand stylist does not stop at using things for their original purpose, which in any case has often vanished in the mists of time. Warming pans, for example, although superseded many times over – by the stone hot water bottle, the rubber bottle, the electric warming pan, then the electric blanket – are still madly popular, purely as decorative objects. But many things can be useful as well as ornamental, especially if you can do a bit of crafty adaptation. The knack of transformation is not to think 'What earthly use is *that*?' but to appreciate something for its shape, material, colour or whatever, and then devise a use for it. Many of these buys should be dirt cheap, as both the dealer and other shoppers, less imaginative than you, will have written them off as useless.

Furniture
This is a rich field for transformation scenes. One very popular ploy (which unfortunately quite a lot of people have already

84

tumbled to, thus raising the market price) is to use old treadle sewing-machine stands to make a table. These stands are beautiful, made of black-painted cast iron and ornately patterned. Some people leave the foot-operated treadle plate in place (working it up and down has a curiously soothing effect); others remove it, along with the wheel, for a less cluttered look. One of these makes a support for a small side table (the top could be an oval of plate glass, or a slab of secondhand marble); a pair make an ideal base for a dining table. I have one with a 6ft long top made from chipboard covered with green and scarlet tiles and framed in pine.

Hall stands usually go cheap because people don't have room in their halls for them any more. They consist of an upper frame incorporating a mirror, where the hats and coats were hung, and a base usually containing a small drawer with umbrella-draining spaces below. One of these formed the basis of my first kitchen, acting as a mini-dresser. I fixed narrow shelves to the back of the upper part, with hooks on their undersides for mugs, and put a worktop on the base, enclosing this with hardboard side panels and sliding doors to make a cupboard. If you don't feel up to all this they look very attractive brightly painted, with the panels set off with floral

wallpaper, and can be used to display a collection of pot plants.

Suppose you need a coffee table? They are not common in junk shops because they are a relatively modern invention. But once you start thinking in terms of cutting short the legs of other tables all sorts of possibilities open up.

It is also possible to cut down a chest of drawers. Removing the bottom drawer from a four-drawer chest considerably reduces its height and makes it look more at home in a low-ceilinged modern room. (A power jig-saw is advisable, otherwise it's hard sledding.) Pine chests of drawers can also be parleyed into very convincing kitchen dressers. Take out the bottom, full-width drawers, and remove the feet, if any. Fit a pair of doors – the easiest type to make consist of vertical tongue and groove boards, strapped across the back; I can do these, somewhat to my surprise. If you are more skilled you can make panelled doors. Then make a set of shelves to go on top, equipped with a suitably curved fascia board.

Many Edwardian wardrobes were made to be dismantled for easy carriage, and a big one can yield several pieces of furniture for the price of one, with the aid of some very basic carpentry. Again, few people now have the space for these large pieces – a fact reflected in the price. They are usually made of beautiful wood such as mahogany, with matched-veneer panels, and sometimes painted or inlaid decorations. What can be done depends on the design of the piece, but a typical yield might be a coffee-table-cum-seat from the base plinth; a stereo cabinet or storage chest from the doors; a settle from the main body of the wardrobe and its bottom drawer; and a storage unit from the fitted section of the wardrobe.

Old dressing tables can be treated in a similar fashion. The tilting mirror can be removed for hanging; the small pair of drawers on top make a useful desk tidy placed one on top of the other; the base can be kept as a chest of drawers, or cut down to make a telephone seat.

Drawers alone have lots of possibilities, if you take them out and turn them this way and that. A small drawer (say an unwanted one from an old hall stand) can be fitted with shelves to make an 'antique' spice rack. A medium-sized one, painted white and fitted with shelves and two large mirror tiles sliding in plastic track becomes a bathroom cabinet. A pair of larger ones, fitted with brass corners and drop handles, makes a handsome military chest.

Simply turning things the wrong way round can give them new uses. A boring full-length mirror, turned sideways, could form the basis of a glamorous 'star's dressing room' make-up unit. A poky single-door wardrobe that holds little but dominates a small bedroom might be more useful laid down on its back and given a foam slab top to become an extra seating unit, with storage for guest bedding inside.

China and glass

China and glass that is long past its best days, and too unhygienic to use, can be employed in a lot more ways than the simply decorative. Keen indoor gardeners, constantly potting up cuttings and acquiring new plants, have an insatiable need for old saucers to stand the pots on, and small bowls or jugs to make *cache pots* to hide boring plastic pots. Small flowering plants look very pretty in a large old breakfast cup and saucer (but you need to be brave enough to drill a drainage hole in the bottom – use a sharp masonry bit and a slow speed; work through a piece of masking tape to stop the drill wandering).

When it comes to bulbs, no drainage holes are necessary if bulb fibre is used, so absolutely anything can be pressed into service, from bowls, mugs, sauce boats and teapots to the now somewhat hackneyed chamber-pot. (If you think that's twee, I once frequented a seaside pub which boasted a floral display planted in a Victorian lavatory pan.) And an old-fashioned long-spouted coffee pot *sans* lid is perfect for watering bulbs and houseplants; much prettier than the hardware store's plastic horrors.

Come summer containers for flowers become a pressing need which junk china can amply fill. I much prefer china to glass as I don't like to see the stems below, especially when, neglected by me, they are turning green and furry. If a favourite vase leaks because it is badly cracked, finish the job by plunging it into boiling water, then mend as described on page 78. If it's suffering from multiple cracks either place a cheap plastic container inside, or relegate it to dried flower display work.

Old dinner plates are commonly collected for their decorative value, but they also make good house number plates (pun intended). You need a round plate with a wide decorated rim and a plain centre on which to paint your house number or name. Again drilling is involved, to enable it to be screwed in place on the house wall. Artistically done, the end result resembles one of those expensive made-to-order pottery house plaques, at a fraction of the cost.

There is nothing new in turning ornate vases and jugs into lamp bases, but you can do it with something much humbler than Ming. Old stoneware jars that even I would hesitate to use for liquids any longer, because of the impossibility of cleaning them properly and suspicions about what they may have been used for in the past, look splendid fitted with simple open-weave fabric drum shades. Conversion to take a light bulb is easy, as you can buy special fittings designed for just this purpose, with tapered bases allowing them to be fitted to different sizes of neck. Stone jars are usually heavy enough to stand safely on their own, but others should have some sand or pebbles put inside to counteract top-heaviness.

Most of the above applies equally well to old glass containers, but don't overlook the possibilities of empty bottles. Although these are in the main purely ornamental (see Chapter 5) they can also be useful. Lamps made from straw-covered chianti bottles suffered from over-popularity in the fifties and were *out*, but now that all things fiftyish are vogueish perhaps they are *in*. But there are plenty of other bottles to choose from. The bigger the bottle the more impressive-looking the lamp, so a lamp-making project is a great excuse for buying a two-litre bottle of something exotic. Pubs are a good source of large or fancy bottles. I once begged a huge (gallon-size) triangular-shaped whisky bottle from an obliging landlord, which became by turns a bedside lamp and a bottle garden. Pubs often keep obscure liqueurs packaged in the most amazing bottles; but the trouble is that such stuff doesn't sell very fast, and there is a temptation to hurry things along by constantly popping in for nips oneself.

The large traditional Italian chianti bottles which have a spout and an inner receptacle for ice are useful for serving cocktails as well as being highly decorative. (Incidentally, martinis taste infinitely better if mixed in advance and left for the ingredients to mature and mingle. Recipe: pour in 1 bottle Cinzano Bianco, ½ bottle of gin and add the zest of a lemon. Leave at least overnight before drinking; the longer it's left the better it tastes. Serve iced.)

If you have one of those bottle-chopping devices, old bottles can be turned into all sorts of things, from ash trays to vases. They also make beautifully Dickensian-looking candle lanterns for taking carol singing or to hang in the garden for a summer party, on bonfire night or at Hallowe'en. Cut the top and bottom out of a green wine bottle and sit the resulting cylinder of glass inside a small tin can. An arrangement of bent coat-hanger wire hooked into holes punched on four sides of the tin enables the lantern to be hung up. And if you go in for the sort of parties where the glass breakage rate tends to be high, flat-bottomed bottles make good, if somewhat crude glasses that are hard to smash. Be careful to smooth the rims thoroughly with emery cloth.

Fabric and yarn

The classic way of transforming old textiles is to cut them up into hexagons and other shapes to make patchwork quilts. Not many of us have time for that nowadays, but machine patchwork, using square or rectangular patches, is far quicker, and an attractive way of making small items like waistcoats or cushion covers for virtually nothing.

Another popular craft in the good old, bad old days was making rugs out of rags; such rugs were often the only floor coverings that very poor families had. In Britain the most popular sort was made by cutting the rags up into strips and knotting them on to a piece of sacking with a latch hook, the kind used for making rugs with wool. In Colonial America those made by plaiting long strips of rag and sewing them into a circle were more popular. Rising affluence has lead to an almost total demise of the rag rug, but the way things are going they could be making a come-back any time now. Anyway, if you are a thriftily-minded young homemaker with bare boards in the bedrooms and some time on your hands you might like to try your hand at it, and keep the craft alive.

Strips of rag, together with chunky yarn, can also be used for coarse weaving. You don't need a loom for this; just stretch string up and down an old picture frame to form the warp, then weave the rags and yarn over and under to form the weft. The idea is to produce something multi-coloured and exaggeratedly hand-made looking, to make into the sort of cushion cover that looks as if it grew rather than having been made.

A lot of the knitwear around in charity shops is too far gone to wear, but can be bought for recycling if it is not hopelessly felted. Freshly unravelled yarn is just one mass of kinks; to straighten it out wind it into skeins, not balls – the quickest way to do this is to get someone to sit still for you with their two hands raised, and wind the yarn loosely between them; otherwise make do with the back of a chair. Then wash the skein and dry, when all kinks should have disappeared.

Some knitwear can be adapted more simply by those who, like me, can only *just* knit. For example you could remove the sleeves from an out-at-the-elbows sweater and use some of the yarn to knit a ribbing on to the armhole and turn it into a slipover. The arms of a chunky knitted garment might make a good pair of legwarmers if you cut them off and knitted on some ribbing. A child's sweater can be turned into a woolly hat for a man or big-headed woman: cut off the body under the arms, gather up the cut edge and draw it up tightly on the wrong side; finish with a pompom made from the rest of the wool.

Old yarn is also useful if you are learning to knit, as you needn't feel inhibited about wasting wool. Knitting up a lot of squares is good for developing that facility with needles that makes garments grow quickly, and for learning to keep an even tension. Use at least 5mm knitting needles and yarns of approximately the same thickness; 20 x 10cm squares are a convenient size. Stocking stitch is easy to do (1 row plain, 1 row purl) and looks good if the squares are assembled so that the wrong (ridged) side is on the top. Another use for old yarn is to practise fancy stitches. Now that knitting patterns are getting so much more ambitious than they used to be, it's handy to know how to do things like picot tuck stitch, fishtail,

open twisted rib and eye of the lynx. (Don't expect me to tell
you how they're done; such knitting is way beyond my
abilities. Borrow a knitting manual from the library.) Practice
pieces can be assembled to make a knitting sampler, like the
old sewing samplers that were originally made as 'pattern
books' for copying, as well as testifying to some poor girl's skill
with the needle.

Superannuated fabrics and yarns both have lots of uses in
relation to children. Thinking about practising knitting
reminds me that as a very small child I used to get endless fun
out of a knitting nancy. If you've never heard of this, in my day
it was a cotton reel with a row of nails knocked in around the
top, but nowadays you can buy smart plastic ones complete
with instructions. The knitting nancy magically produces a
multi-coloured woollen worm which can then be coiled round
and sewn up to make dubious gifts for grown-ups, such as
grubby potholders and table mats.

Soft toys made out of old wool are appealing to small
children since they are particularly soft and cuddly. They can
take part in making them too, for even very small children can
knit squares and rectangles, or a miniature scarf. These can be
made either out of recycled wool or by cutting up old woollies,
the more felted the better. You don't really need patterns for
these toys. Simple squares and rectangular shapes serve for
bodies, heads and legs, and the character of whatever animal
it's supposed to be is achieved by the proportions, colour of the
wool and accessories like a mane or tail. If it still ends up
looking like nothing on earth, that's exactly what it is – a
relative of E.T's. Fortunately children have remarkable
powers of imagination!

Rag dolls are fun to make; patterns for them turn up
regularly in women's magazines and in the backs of dressmaking pattern books, or get a book on the subject. Rag dolls are
often far more popular with children than super-real vinyl ones
that walk, talk and do god-knows what else, partly because
they love things made by parents rather than bought. Another
advantage of rag dolls is that it's not hopelessly expensive to
make a large one, which can be dressed in the child's own
cast-off clothing. (Tip: cut-up old nylon tights help make

stuffing go further.) Soft toy animals are often made in fur fabric, which is quite expensive to buy; what better source of supply than a tatty old fur-fabric coat?

Craft shops and haberdashery counters stock all sorts of little items that make home-made toys more elegant and amusing, such as bells for horses' reins and growlers for teddy bears (see Useful Addresses, page 126).

As well as being made into toys, old dresses, hats and shoes *are* toys in themselves. A dressing-up box used to be part of every middle-class household's equipment, and can still hold more lure than the television when the mood is right. And an old blanket or bedspread stretched over a washing line makes a splendid tent which will keep small children amused outdoors for hours.

Old equipment

Outdated or unwanted industrial, household and agricultural equipment has many uses. A classic example is the acid carboy; these enormous cloudy-green glass jars used to make splendid bottle gardens, but genuine ones are few and far between these days, and too highly sought after to be cheap. Another trendy item is the printer's typecase, a many-compartmented wooden box formerly used for holding metal letters which the printer plucked out with tweezers in the days of hand-setting. Long-since superseded, they make delightful display cases for small ornaments.

Items you are more likely to get your hooks on include old sinks. Genuine old stone ones are rare, but common white glazed ones can be faked up to look like stone, and then turned into alpine gardens. This is done with a substance called hypertufa, made from cement, sand and sieved peat. Mix these together with just enough water to bind, in the proportions of one part each of cement and two parts peat. Apply the mixture to the sink one side at a time, first painting it with PVA (woodworking) adhesive to make the hypertufa stick. While it is still soft roughen it up to get a stone-like appearance. It won't look very natural at first, but quickly weathers in a very satisfying way.

Other objects that can be put to good use in the garden are

old wooden wheelbarrows; nobody wants these any more because they are amazingly heavy, even before you have filled them to overflowing with weeds or prunings. Painted and planted with bright annual flowers they can look charming in the right setting. Old chimney pots are priceless now that large earthenware flower pots cost a small fortune, even the plain ones. Stoneware drainpipes have possibilities, too – I have one supporting a bird bath which was made by coating an old galvanised iron dustbin lid with stone paint. There is also a way of turning illegally treadless car tyres into flower urns, which I must admit I have not grappled with, but I gather it demands considerable brute strength as it involves slitting them open and turning them inside out. I acquired mine from a previous garden; people usually paint them white, but this one has been left *au naturel*, and the dark grey rubber looks quite like the expensive lead used for urns in stately homes, though lacking moulded garlands and cherubs. Yet another possible flower container is an old milk churn, should one come your way. Being tall, they get the flower display up nice and high. They will rust, so should be wire brushed and painted with red lead paint before you do any decorative work.

One more garden idea: vintage wooden ladders are even less sought after than wheelbarrows, as a woodwormed rung could be fatal. But they make ideal supports for twining garden climbers like clematis and honeysuckle. Use a single one horizontally, as part of a pergola or screen; a pair could form the basis of a decorative arch.

Back inside, old doors can be transformed into highly functional desks. The best kind are veneered flush ones, which can form the top more or less as they are. Cheap hardboard-faced ones need covering with vinyl 'leather' or laminated plastic. Old panelled ones can also be used, but you have first to pack the panels up level with the frame and then cover with hardboard. If the door is longer than you wish the desk to be simply cut it down. Modern flush doors only have a paper honeycomb core inside, and so are easy to cut. Remove the timber trim from the end and replace it to cover the cut edge. The base of the desk can be a pair of low filing cabinets; an old typist's desk or dressing table; or rest one end on a batten screwed to the wall and the other on a cheap drawer or cupboard unit. Small desks can be supported by a heavyweight proprietary slotted upright and metal bracket system, but are never as stable as one in contact with the floor.

Some items can be used for purposes closer to their original ones. For example, you might come across a pair of old bee-keeper's bellows (to blow smoke into the hive, which makes the bees think there's a fire and leave smartly, enabling the keeper to collect the honey; sneaky, isn't it?) They are just as good at coaxing embers into a blaze, nearly as decorative as proper fire bellows and should cost far less. Also look for antique cistern brackets, the curly wrought-iron jobs that used to support the old-fashioned high-level lavatory cisterns which were operated by pulling a chain instead of daintily pressing a lever or button. What am I saying, 'used to' – there are still plenty of these antique beasts around Britain, particularly in public lavatories and pubs. Anyway, these brackets are immensely strong – they had to be, to support a heavy metal cistern *and* two gallons of water – and make good supports for shelves intended to hold a lot of weight (but the shelf must be thick too, say 1in (25mm) timber, and/or the brackets placed close together). If you only have one odd bracket paint it matt black or glossy white and use it to support a hanging flower basket.

Secondhand items which can be put to new uses come from many different periods of time and different parts of the world. Old brass shellcases from the First World War used to be very popular, and were polished up and used to hold fire irons or flowers. Nowadays wooden bobbins from long-closed-down textile mills in the north of England are turning up in smart shops as skipping rope handles, popular in the current health and fitness craze. These same shops have prettily painted tiny metal tins, which used to hold steel needles in the days of the wind-up gramophone.

The message is: practically anything can be turned to a new use if you put your mind to it.

7 FIXTURES AND FITTINGS

If you buy a Victorian or Edwardian house you will probably find, as you get better acquainted with it and its neighbours in the street, that many of the features it should possess have been ripped out by previous modernisers. Where there should be a graceful panelled front door, ideally with stained glass lights, there may be anything from flush plywood to aluminium and glass or one of those Philippine mahogany fake Georgian affairs. Interior doors, too, have frequently been replaced with modern flush types; and both are almost bound to have the wrong door furniture, whether it's cheap plastic or expensive but over-ornate brass. The original small-paned sash windows may have been reglazed or replaced, turned spindles and curving mahogany banister rails removed from the stairway, elegant cast iron or marble fireplace surrounds ousted by clumsy porridge-coloured ceramic-tiled monsters.

For many of these items the only place to get replacements at all, or to get them without spending a fortune, is on the secondhand market, which means mainly from demolition contractors, who salvage anything and everything from the buildings they knock down.

If your house is modern, secondhand fixtures and fittings can give it a much-needed bit of character. And for DIY enthusiasts secondhand timber, roofing materials, doors and windows can drastically cut the cost of building a home extension or garage, or of putting up fences or pergolas.

Doors are what the average demolition yard has in greatest quantity. Absolutely any kind is likely to turn up. Not just house doors of every date and description, from run-of-the-mill painted softwood to solid oak with ornate carving, but garage doors, louvre doors, cupboard doors, conservatory doors. Finding exactly what you want in the right size may take time, hunting among hundreds stacked anyhow, but it should be in there somewhere. Panelled doors suitable for Victorian terrace houses have become rather highly sought after in London in recent years, so don't pay too much. A stripped pine panelled internal door should not cost much more than £20 (a new one sells for about £40). But an Edwardian front door with stained glass panels might be nearer £50. Hardwood doors naturally cost more than softwood.

If your doors have survived but it's fittings you need, these too should be available, more cheaply than reproduction ones from a specialist supplier, whether you require china or wooden knobs, black iron or brass.

As well as doors a large yard should have lots of other timber items: moulded architraves and skirtings, panelling, wooden shutters, shelving and other former shop fitments, and decorative items like broken pediments and pilasters to enhance a doorway. For staircase renovation you should be able to get everything from a single spindle to replace one missing or broken, to complete sets, banister rails, newel posts, and even whole staircases.

Fireplace surrounds are another common item, in cast iron, carved wood and even marble (or slate painted to look like marble). Many of these were ripped out many years ago by house-owners desiring something modern – the appalling ceramic tiled lumps – others went later when the central heating boom began and no one wanted fireplaces any more. In those days they were cheap because no one loved them; now they can be quite expensive, as many people now want an open fire as well as central heating, and are more concerned than they were to have something in keeping with the period of the house. Cheap ones are likely to be rather small and mean – the ones that originally came out of bedrooms.

Overmantels were a popular adjunct to the Victorian fireplace. They usually consist of a mirror framed with a gothic-style hardwood surround incorporating lots of ledges and shelves for displaying the bric-a-brac of which the Victorians were so inordinately fond. As well as providing the finishing touch to your authentic Victorian fire surround these can be useful in other places. I once had a rather rococo one, covered with carved bows and swags, painted white and installed over the bathroom washbasin. It provided the biggest mirror I've ever had plus lots of storage space for bathroom clutter. A plainer one, in mahogany with carved art nouveau lilies, was ideal in a small dark hall, reflecting light and providing a useful shelf.

The sturdy and highly decorative ceramic tiles, sometimes

hand-painted, that often formed the hearth as well as part of the fire surround have become collectable and thus expensive. You are unlikely to find exactly the same pattern and colour to replace one cracked or missing, but even if they don't match they should blend in.

Another treasure you might come across in this area is an original cast iron cylindrical stove of the kind now very expensive to buy new.

Some demolition contractors have a lot of fittings from old churches, which can be put to good use if you like something really unusual in your home, and don't mind spending a bit of money. Stained-glass window panels can replace boring obscure glass on landings, in halls or in bathrooms, or be used as screens to divide up room areas, or to stand in fireplaces during the summer. Old pews, delightful though they are, are rather on the gargantuan side to use as seating in the average home, but make magnificent garden benches. Church railings and other decorative ironwork must have a use somewhere, though I haven't found one myself, yet . . .

On a more mundane level, demolition yards abound with superannuated sanitary fittings: baths, basins and loos. Sometimes they have dozens of exactly the same model, presumably dating from the demolition or modernisation of a hotel. Many of them are unusable as they are chipped or cracked, defects which cannot be remedied. But if sound, a large white washbasin might be a good buy, to replace one of the small mean models builders like to inflict on us nowadays. The basin should be cheap, but installing it might cost a lot more unless you can do it yourself. This is a simple job – I've done it, and if I can you can – provided the tap holes are the same distance apart as on the original one, so that pipework does not have to be altered.

I can't believe that anyone really wants an old freestanding bath with claw feet; but some people will do anything to be different. I once knew a man with an enormous garden who had several of these discreetly positioned around the plot, which enabled him to continue watering his precious plants throughout the hottest, driest summers when the authorities always ban the use of hosepipes just as you need them most.

As for old loos: provided they are not hopelessly lime-scaled and stained, as well as cracked or chipped, they are perfectly hygienic. An ornate Victorian one in working order would certainly be a talking point; whether you want to go the whole hog and also have an overhead cistern mounted on curly cast-iron brackets and operated by a pull-chain is up to you. To make the picture complete you would need a Victorian washbasin, ornately decorated and incorporating such joys as a scallop overflow and shell soap dishes. In 1982 a famous British manufacturer of sanitary pottery brought out a new range called the Imperial collection, which features copies of basins and lavatory pans like these, at prices ranging from £245 to £375. So by shopping at a demolition yard you could be in the swim for considerably less.

Whether your loo is ancient or modern, a wooden seat is a comfortable addition. I don't care whether they are now thought to be the last word in chic, or hopelessly *passé* (depends where you live); I can tell you from experience that they are much more warm and welcoming to the bare anatomy on a cold morning than modern plastic. So a vintage one, be it humble pine or classy mahogany with brass fittings, is a real find – a new mahogany one costs a minimum of £40, and over £60 if you go to the wrong place. However dubious they look they can soon be rendered clean and safe for use by thorough sanding and plenty of varnish.

Some demolition contractors, the smarter ones operating under cover rather than just from a yard, may also have an assortment of furniture, pictures and books; anything that happened to be around during demolition work. They can be a cheaper source of supply than regular shops, or at least a source of some interesting finds. Others may also have a line in items taken from gardens: flower urns, pots and boxes, and statuary in stone, lead and bronze.

Finally demolition yards of every sort are the place to go for cheap building materials; or when secondhand items are preferable to new ones, for example when making roof repairs. As well as timber of all descriptions there are likely to be slates, tiles, bricks, chimney pots, roof trusses and sheet materials such as plasterboard and corrugated iron or asbestos.

RESTORATION WORK

Items bought from a demolition contractor are often in a sorry state, having lain out in the rain, or at best in a cold damp shed, perhaps for several years. But with the aid of power sanding equipment, strong chemicals, lots of elbow grease and determination, wonders can be worked on even the most unpromising. Industrial gloves will help to preserve your lily-white hands, and for some jobs goggles are advisable to protect your eyes from flying debris, and a face mask to prevent your lungs from silting up with sanding dust. If all this hasn't put you off, read on.

Old timber

Floorboards and other pieces of softwood invariably have dangerous nails still in them, so get rid of these first. Use a claw hammer or pincers, slipping a piece of hardboard underneath the tool where it presses against the wood if you don't want to mark it. Nails that just won't come out can be worked to and fro until metal fatigue makes them break off. Cut out any rotten bits and burn them, just in case it's dry rot. Always be on the look out for woodworm, and never store secondhand timber in a roof space that has not been sprayed against woodworm, as if there is any worm in the timber it will hatch out and start destroying the rafters. Whenever old timber is used for structural purposes it's as well to give it a precaution-ary brushing with anti-woodworm fluid.

To remove the top layer of damaged and grey-coloured wood from planed timber use a disc sander fitted with coarse abrasive paper, in a electric drill. If at all possible work out of doors so that sanding dust blows away. Unplaned (fuzzy looking) timber is cheap, and adequate for outdoor work and hidden structures. It can be rendered smooth by planing, but this is hard work unless you have a power planer.

Old timber which has been creosoted can be painted if first sealed with shellac varnish.

Doors and panelling

Doors are usually heavily painted, and the easiest course is to send them to a stripping tank. This is quite satisfactory for doors you are going to paint; cost is £8-10. But if you want a clear finish it's best to use one of the DIY methods outlined on pages 23-4, as tank stripping can permanently dull the wood, and may also loosen old animal glue that's holding joints together. Do not send doors with stained-glass lights, and remove door furniture first.

Matching up missing stained glass is skilled work. Look in the Yellow Pages under Stained Glass Suppliers. If that fails contact CoSIRA (see page 126) who may be able to put you in touch with a local craftsman.

A secondhand door can be planed down *slightly*, if necessary, in order to fit your door frame, but not very much or its proportions would be ruined. Enlarging it a little by pinning and gluing on strips of wood is possible, but will always show even if painted over, as eventually differential movement of the pieces cracks the paint film down the join. On an exterior door this opens the way for water to get in.

New door furniture to smarten up any style of door can be bought from specialist suppliers (see page 126). Brass is beautiful but horrendously expensive so you'll be pleased to hear that black iron is usually more correct for front doors. Also it does not need constant polishing; though you can always resort to lacquering old brass fittings,which is common-ly already done on new ones.

Fittings

Removing unwanted fittings from doors or other items can be hard going, and if you go about it the wrong way you can totally fail to budge them, or do so much damage in the process that the item is scarred for life. Squirt rusted-in screws or bolts with penetrating and easing oil and leave for a few hours for it to soak in. Clear the slots of overpainted screws before trying to turn them. Use a screwdriver that fits the width of the slot *exactly*, and push *hard* as you give the first turn – once the screw moves, even a fraction, it will then go the rest of the way. But if it won't shift, and the edges of the slot get mashed as you keep trying, it's probably there for good. Other methods to break the grip of locked-in fixings are heat – apply the tip of a soldering iron or red-hot poker; shock – hit the screwdriver or spanner with a mallet; and counter-attack – try turning it the wrong way. If all these tricks fail you can try a tool called a screw extractor, or attempt to drill it out. Otherwise chisel round the head so you can grip it with pliers.

If you have a great many stubborn old screws to get out it's worth buying a special screwdriver: either one with a large ball handle, or one with a detachable ratchet handle, both of which give considerably increased torque.

When the boot is on the other foot and it's the fittings you want, such as splendid old hinges or a black iron door knocker, obviously it doesn't matter too much what damage is done to the wood. I have even salvaged heavy hinges and bolts from a rotten garden gate by burning it and then raking them out of the ashes, thus killing two birds with one stone as the heat had burnt the old paint off them.

Normally old paint can be removed from metal or china fittings very easily with liquid chemical stripper, especially if they can be submerged in it. Clean up iron fittings as described below; for brass use steel wool and metal polish. Paint iron fittings with satin black rather than gloss or matt.

Rust

Items such as iron and steel firedogs, baskets and fire irons are likely to be badly rusted. Severe attacks need the attentions of a wire brush in a power tool. This is drastic treatment; a slightly gentler approach is to use an abrasive flap wheel in a power tool. Light surface rust can be sanded away by hand using emery paper. An alternative method is to use a patent rust remover, which is painted on and rinsed off. This is particularly good for cistern brackets or other ornamental ironwork where the convolutions of the surface prevent the use of sanding tools. If items are to be painted give them an undercoat of anti-rust primer first.

Old grates can be black-leaded, just as they were in the past. Or, for a permanent finish that looks very similar, paint with heat-resisting black paint thinned with white spirit.

If rust has actually eaten a hole in something repair with a glass-fibre kit sold for car body work, following instructions.

Rust stains on baths, basins, concrete, stone and tiles can be removed with proprietary rust remover, which will also remove heavy tarnish from copper, brass, bronze or aluminium fittings.

Fireplace surrounds

Remove any rust from a cast-iron fireplace as described above. If old paint is flaking strip off with liquid stripper; otherwise rub down with abrasive paper. Paint with black heat-resisting paint if the fireplace is to be used; otherwise gloss paint will do, in any colour you fancy.

Treat marble fireplace surrounds as described on page 21. Some apparently marble surrounds turn out on close inspection to be slate painted in marble effect. If this has chipped in places it can be touched up with an artist's brush and gloss paints. But often such surrounds were over-painted when chips appeared. It is theoretically possible to remove the paint without disturbing the marble effect below by gentle use of paint stripper; but tedious and uncertain. You might prefer to take off the lot and have a slate fire surround.

Clean and repair a wooden fireplace surround just as if it

were a piece of furniture, but finish with a matt polyurethane varnish rather than anything glossy.

Outdoor stone and earthenware

Items like urns and statues should be cleaned as little as possible. They are often made of rather soft stone in the first place, such as sandstone or limestone, and natural growths of lichen, as well as being part of their antique charm, form a protective crust that softens the effect of wind and rain. Harsh scrubbing can cause the stone below to crumble away. If such an item really is dirty, confine yourself to prolonged hosing down and light brushing.

Granite and basalt are much harder and smoother and can take much rougher treatment: wash in soap and water and if necessary scrub.

Repairs to stonework can be done with epoxy resin adhesive, and missing pieces of small dimensions can be built up by mixing the adhesive with powdered stone.

Old terracotta pots are great treasures as modern ones are ridiculously expensive, being mostly imported. They are easily cleaned by scrubbing in plenty of water; a little bleach added to the water will help to prevent green stains reappearing. Handle carefully; they are heavy but brittle. Mend breaks with PVA woodworking adhesive. Do not leave such pots out in the winter as frost can shatter them. (This is why containers for bonsai trees are even more costly, as they are made of specially fired ceramic ware that will stand up to frost.)

Lead

Window boxes or statues made from lead, although heavy, are easily damaged as it is a very soft metal, so take great care when moving such items. A dull grey look is the right thing for lead; it should not be shiny. Remove dirt with gentle scrubbing in plain water; scouring powder is permissible if absolutely necessary. Corrosion turns lead white, and an item with heavy attacks would need to be treated with a weak solution of hydrochloric acid, washed off with a weak ammonium acetate followed by plain water.

8 WHERE TO LOOK

Before starting on *where*, how about the crunch question: How much to pay? With new goods this is no problem, as recommended retail prices set a known standard which you then seek to beat by shopping around. You are also able to compare like with like, and this year's price with last.

In the secondhand world there is no such thing as value. If no one wants a particular item it is worth nothing. If it suddenly becomes fashionable, and everybody and his mother wants it, the same object could be worth hundreds of pounds. And even then there is never a fixed price, only a point of compromise between what the seller hopes to get and the buyer is prepared to pay. Price is also affected by geography; the same piece of china will fetch far more in the Portobello Road than it would in a jumble sale in the Outer Hebrides. Time is another factor: the seller may want a quick sale even at a low price, or be prepared to wait for a higher offer.

There are two main ways of keeping your sanity in this madhouse. If, like me, you are buying things for use, rather than aiming to become a collector or acquire investments, your constant source of comparison must be the same object if bought new. Of course, few secondhand items, except such things as fairly recent cookers and refrigerators (cars are the classic example) will be exactly the same as their brand-new counterparts. But comparison with the same *sort* of object is enough to enable you to keep your feet on the ground and not

pay more for a secondhand item, except in a few rare cases where there is a good reason for doing so.

Your second protection is simply knowledge. As you gain experience of shopping secondhand style you will develop a similar instinct to the dealers for what is a fair price. Their knowledge is encyclopedic; you only have to worry about the things you happen to be interested in. Actually they get a lot of their knowledge from *Lyle's Guide*, which you too can dip into at the library. This lists the prices paid at auction the previous year for a vast range of antiques and collectables; every item is illustrated, so it can be a great help if you think you have made a real find.

Finally, never lose track of whether you actually *like* whatever it is you are buying. I have seen dealers falling over themselves to bid several hundred pounds for a hideous black Victorian bookcase plastered with bulbous carvings which I would not have taken as a gift.

Some people are put off buying secondhand by the business of bargaining. You don't *have* to, and in some places it is not the done thing (see below). But no dealer will respect you for paying the asking price – he'll just put you down in his memory as an idiot, and look for you again. Once you get the hang of it, bargaining is all part of the fun.

Crudely, bargaining goes like this. You ask the dealer what he's asking for X, he gives you a hugely inflated figure, you indicate shock, despair, astonishment and offer half that.

Eventually you settle on a price which will probably be what he expected to get all the time. When a dealer refuses to play it is because he knows he will eventually find a buyer at the asking price – and you can always try again next week if he hasn't.

Once you have dabbled a toe or two in the waters and learnt to enjoy bargaining, buying secondhand style makes ordinary shopping seem very tame.

Antique fairs and flea markets

Some of these are very smart, with prices to match, but others are more down to earth – 'up-market secondhand' fairs rather than true antique fairs – so you might just find the odd bargain there, particularly late in the day. Like market stall holders, dealers at fairs rent a stall for the day, and would rather sell something for a small profit than pack it up and cart it home.

Antique fairs are held variously in hotels, halls and former cinemas; most are strictly commercial but some are wholly or partly for charity. A charge may be made for admittance, but it's usually only 50p or so. Some of the tattier ones call themselves flea markets, although on the Continent this means a regular open-air market specialising in secondhand clothes and other junk.

How to find   Small ads in local papers; *Exchange and Mart*.

Auctions

At first visit an auction room seems a frightening, dangerous place; a mysterious closed world which you can never hope to understand. But once you have been to a few you'll soon begin to understand what's going on, and pluck up the courage to join in. The thrill of making a successful bid, of snatching the desired lot from the jaws of the opposition, is what makes buying at an auction so much fun. And where else could you find such a rich variety of goods: an eighteenth-century Chinese armorial mug (no home complete without one); a 92-piece Victorian Worcester dinner service; an ancient violin and a modern Hoover; a Hornby train set and a Patagonian nose flute, all in the same room on the same day?

Most bidders at any auction are dealers, who make their

living at the game and are aware of the likely price of everything from vast Edwardian wardrobes to dainty pieces of Coalport. How can you make a successful bid against this pack of experts, without simply paying over the odds? For two reasons: first, because you are buying for yourself, whereas they have to allow for a profit margin of anything up to 100 per cent. Second, their criteria are different from yours: you are looking for something you *like*, whereas they are looking for what will sell. But beware of being 'run up'. If a group of dealers get nettled because you are depriving them of their profits by buying direct, they may bid against you and push the price up to what you would have had to pay if you *had* bought

from them. So the golden rule of auction buying is to decide positively in advance what your top limit is, and not get carried away by auction fever.

The main snag about buying at an auction is that it is time-consuming. In order to inspect goods carefully you need to attend the viewing, usually the day before; and on the day, items you are interested in may be widely spaced out through a list of hundreds of lots which will take the auctioneer several hours to get through.

Go to the viewing armed with a catalogue (from 20p for a duplicated list, to a pound or more for a printed job with pictures) and a tape measure to check sizes – impossibly huge pieces of furniture can look deceptively small in the company of other, similar elephants. Mark anything you are interested in and make a note of any defects you spot, and what you are prepared to pay. All the items will be numbered, and on the day the auctioneer goes through them in strict order. So if you covet lot 295 you don't need to turn up in time for lot 1. Auctioneers reckon to whistle through about 120 lots each hour, so you can work out fairly precisely when to appear. Some lots bear the mysterious letters 'a.f.' after the description. This is a somewhat vague term, standing for 'as found', and appears to indicate the presence of some serious defect, or lack of knowledge on the auctioneer's part as to whether it actually works.

When it comes to bidding forget all those stories about people scratching their noses and being lumbered with six diamond rings. You are far more likely to fail to register with the auctioneer because you are too hesitant, too slow, hidden behind a pillar or because he doesn't recognise you as a bidding face. Copy the dealers' technique: they make a first bid with a positive gesture, then signify they are still bidding by a discreet flip of the catalogue or nod of the head. As they drop out they just shake their heads or turn away.

Bidding normally rises in £2-£3 steps for low-value items (£30, £32, £35, £38, £40), and in £5 or £10 steps for more expensive lots. The starting price is set by the auctioneer: not so low as to prolong bidding, not so high as to deter an initial bid. Do not jump in too quickly as first bidder; if there is a deathly hush the auctioneer will lower the starting price. At some auctions a list is prepared showing the prices expected for each lot; these are pretty accurate and a quick look may save you wasting time waiting around only to find that bidding pushes the price of an item way beyond what you personally are prepared to pay. Auction room porters are very knowledgeable and can help you, or even bid for you.

Don't lose sight of the fact that the price upon which the auctioneer's hammer falls is not the end of the story. On top of that you *may* have to pay commission of 5-10 per cent, plus VAT on the commission; so £20 slithers up to £22.30. And if the item is too large for you to get home, allow for transport costs as well. Most auction rooms take cheques these days, for the modest amounts of money we are thinking of spending, so you don't need to have your pockets bulging with fivers.

Finally, do not confuse regular auctions held at reputable

auction rooms with one-day affairs in hotel rooms or church halls. The latter are strictly sucker traps and you should have nothing to do with them.

How to find Yellow Pages, local newspaper ads.

Charity shops

The number of these around has grown enormously over the last few years, reflecting the increasing popularity of buying secondhand. Oxfam has 612 and is opening more all the time; add those run by Help the Aged, War on Want, Shelter, The Spastics Society and various other charities and you should have a good chance of finding at least one in the High Street where you shop.

The Oxfam shops are the best known and they are big business, with an annual turnover of around £12 million (well, not big compared to Woolworth's, but a giant besides Steptoe and Son). They have achieved their success by the happy inclusion of new goods, many made specially for them in developing countries, avoiding the tatty and depressing air which gathers in some such shops. They also have smart shop fronts and attractive window displays.

All this combines to make shopping at Oxfam very like shopping at any other shop, except that the profits are going not to line shareholders' pockets or send the owner's kids to public school, but to help finance Oxfam's tireless efforts to help developing countries help themselves, as well as supplying emergency aid to disaster areas.

Leaving the new goods aside, delightful though they are, the basic stock consists mainly of clothes for men, women and children, plus small household articles, bric-a-brac and books; some shops also have jewellery, watches, silverware and other collectables. All these goods are donated by people living in the area, so the quality will reflect their lifestyles: woollies are discarded more quickly in Westminster than in Wapping, and labels are superior – more Mary Quant, less Marks and Spencer. Selling prices are decided for each shop by the volunteer staff, who aim to make good money while keeping prices low enough to make sure the stock turns over speedily. (If you've ever wondered: unsold clothing goes to Oxfam's recycling depot in Yorkshire.) The volunteers seek expert advice on pricing special items like jewellery and anything else that their whiskers tell them may be valuable. For pricing clothing they use the same method that I have recommended to you: comparison with the price of the same thing if new. Each shop has a list of current average retail prices, and will charge 10-20 per cent of that figure, depending on the kind of area the shop is in, adjusted for the desirability and condition of the actual item.

So you are not terribly likely to find tremendous bargains in an Oxfam shop (as they rightly point out, if attractive items are displayed at too low a price they are pounced upon by canny general dealers for resale). All items are priced; haggling is not really in order, as the proceeds are for such a good cause. Before buying check the goods carefully for any flaws, as prices take these into account, and you cannot return something for a fault you should have spotted.

Other charity shops may be run on slightly different lines, but the same basic principles apply. Some are much more disorganised, many look terribly tatty. But don't be put off, you may find just what you're looking for. Some charity shops do not price the goods; the volunteer in charge will make an on-the-spot decision, probably assessing *you* more than the goods. So don't wear your mink. But all are happy hunting grounds where you can browse as long as you like, and no one will pressure you to buy. If you have one near your home, a weekly pop-in pays good dividends.

How to find Look in the telephone book under names of charities; or in the Yellow Pages under Charitable Organisations. But mainly keep a sharp eye open when shopping; many charity shops operate from temporary premises. Oxfam shops are easy to spot as they all have a smart black and white fascia board.

Demolition contractors

Demolition firms are as varied in character as any other retail establishment. At the bottom end of the market are tiny yards tucked away in back streets, with not much more to offer than scruffy doors, dilapidated timber and chipped washbasins. At the top end is a place like the London Architectural Salvage & Supply Co., whose enormous range of high-quality fixtures and fittings occupies a disused church, plus a former filling station nearby. Here you can also find timber already cut into usable planks, and if you can't face the task of renovating that genuine Victorian fire surround their experts will do it for you. In between these two extremes are many firms doing good business selling ordinary but extremely useful secondhand building materials of all kinds.

Demolition yard staff can be rather uncertain in their pricing, except for items with a well-established market value, like stripped pine doors. For many of them selling the stuff accumulating in the yard is very much a sideline; their real money comes from demolition and plant hire. This can work in your favour (in some places you feel they should be paying *you* to take things away before they no longer have room to move), but equally they may price something on the high side quite inadvertently. So as usual it is up to you to know what you are prepared to pay. When buying timber in any quantity a catalogue giving current new prices is a helpful guide.

How to find   Look in the Yellow Pages under Demolition; see also local newspaper small ads.

Newspaper advertisements

An assortment of secondhand goods, ranging from old shoes to cookers, is advertised by private individuals in local newspapers (some papers don't charge for goods advertised at under £20, and consequently attract a great many entries). Beware the disguised dealer, and be very careful when buying items that could go wrong. See Your Legal Rights, page 122.

Prices asked range from the sublime to the ridiculous. Some people ask enormous sums for a filthy, 20-year-old gas stove; others ask too little because they just want to get rid of whatever it is fast. Getting a bargain means ringing up as soon as you see the advertisement, going round immediately if interested and paying on the nail. You can't expect a private seller to keep anything for you on the basis of a telephone conversation, and if you don't pay straight away you might get gazumped.

Jumble sales

Everyone who knows about jumble saling advises you to get there well before they open, as only first-comers get anything worth having. Being by nature incapable of arriving on time for anything less demanding than a train (and even then I'm the one tearing along the platform while whistles blow) I have not myself managed to make many purchases of note at a jumble sale. But lots of my friends have, and boast about their amazing acquisitions in a most irritating way.

A typical jumble sale looks extremely unpromising. A bare-boarded, barn-like church hall on a rainy winter morning, freezing cold and smelling strongly of heating oil and old shoes, filled with trestle tables piled high with clapped-out clothing, is no place for a faint-hearted pessimist. The successful jumble salor is the lunatic optimist who just knows that something madly chic, in exactly their size, is hiding underneath all the felted woollies and baggy Crimplene; or that at least one of the myriad pairs of fraying flared trousers harbours a forgotten fiver in the back pocket.

Although such finds are unlikely they *do* happen, and even without these strokes of luck you are still quite likely to pick up something interesting, because although clothing is the staple fare, jumble sale organisers take absolutely everything offered, so there's no telling what may turn up.

Every artefact known to man passes through a jumble sale at some stage, it seems, before reaching the town dump (some items several times: people buy something in a fit of euphoria at the Scouts, discover back home why it got thrown out in the first place, and recycle it to the Cricket Club). Quality is low – bent forks, chipped china, 20-year-old dressmaking patterns and copies of the *Readers Digest*, faded hardbacks by long-forgotten authors of high moral tone, much-thumbed paperbacks with pages missing, torn comics and cracked gramophone records. But so are prices – the going rate for anything is usually counted in pence rather than pounds, unless it is something large like furniture or a carpet. (At one jumble sale I got to they had a vast radiogram filling the hall with velvet-toned music, a bargain at only £5, free delivery.) Usually there is an entrance fee, but this is nominal – 5-15p depending on the neighbourhood. Like charity shops, jumble sales reflect the catchment area, so if you are looking for something a little superior it's worth the journey to a smarter part of town.

Jumble sales usually take place on Saturday morning. Arrive before the advertised time to be first in the queue and get the cream. (If you want the *crème de la crème* be one of the organisers – first pick is their perk.) Go armed with plenty of small change so that you can pay the right amount and not have to waste precious moments while a helper, often young and uncertain of its arithmetic, fumbles for change. Speed is the essence of successful jumble saling! For the same reason do not stop to haggle; this is not really on anyway, as prices are so low and it's all in aid of a Good Cause – though if you happened to want something large, like the afore-mentioned radiogram, and it was still there by mid-afternoon, the organisers would probably be only too glad to accept any offer to get rid of it. But you wouldn't be so hard-nosed as to deprive the Girl Guides of a pound or two . . . would you?

How to find Classified ads and Coming Events in local newspapers; shop windows; church notice boards; Sell-Out section of *Time Out*.

Coffee mornings, bring-and-buy sales and bazaars

These functions are organised by worthy people in support of worthy causes. Coffee mornings and bring-and-buy sales are usually held in somebody's house, which is half the attraction as all the local ladies come along to inspect the fund-raiser's decor and furnishings and criticise the coffee. Men are few, except for a hapless local councillor or two who feel it worthwhile to show their faces. It is surprisingly easy to get rid of several pounds without even noticing it, such is the oh-so-genteel pressure on you to buy. First you may be charged 10p to enter; then there's the obligatory coffee, scone or cake. Usually there's a raffle demanding support; all this before you've even caught sight of anything you might want to buy.

Bazaars are not such cosy affairs, as they usually take place in church halls and the like, often in the weeks before Christmas, but they are run on the same general lines.

Secondhand goods are only part of the stock-in-trade of these functions, as they also deal in cakes, preserves, pot plants, home-made calendars and Christmas cards. But it's well worth popping in to see what's going on, as well as to support the Cause or Party, because as with jumble sales, you just never know what might turn up. Most organisers put price tickets on their goods, and as at the jumble sale bargaining is not really in order.

How to find Small ads and Coming Events in the local press; local noticeboards; word of mouth.

Secondhand shops (general, furniture and clothing)

Everyone talks about junk shops, but no shop I've ever seen actually admits to being one. Some call themselves antique shops, when there is nothing inside that remotely qualifies for the title as defined by the British Antique Dealers' Association, that is over a hundred years old. Others are basically secondhand furniture shops, with a larding of junk items, sometimes a lot of new copper or brass ware strung up in the window to make them look 'antique'.

Call them what you will, the best shops, the ones to seek out and visit regularly once found, are those whose owner has an eye for things that are interesting and attractive, regardless of relative antiquity. The kind of shop shown on the cover is the place to browse, rather than somewhere with just one or two supercilious-looking items in the window, or a whole mass of boring stuff that looks as though it's been sitting there gathering dust for years.

Secondhand shops specialising in furniture are often depressing places, containing nothing but modern mass-produced rubbish in a poor state of repair and covered with white rings and cigarette burns. Another drawback of these shops is that as furniture is large, and the premises small, there is not

much in them and your chances of actually finding anything you like are consequentiy low. For those who live in London, Austin's of Peckham Rye is one of the best places to go. It is a vast warehouse, with furniture on three floors, not to mention another branch in the back streets almost as large. They price everything, the stock ranges from quite expensive near-antiques to mundane useful pieces acquired from bankrupt boarding houses, and they will happily deliver. There is also a constantly changing selection of bric-a-brac and cutlery.

Most towns have several secondhand shops specialising in clothes, and their number is increasing all the time now that old is more fashionable than new in certain quarters; no doubt the recession has something to do with it too. Old-fashioned shops dealing mainly in women's and children's wear may still call themselves dress agencies. Those specialising in men's wear rejoice in the title 'wardrobe dealers'.

Bargaining is essential in any shop where they do not put price tags on articles. 'Antique' shops go in for little tags with a price scribbled on in a code known only to the dealer. This will allow him a mark-up of anything up to 100 per cent, so he really expects to be beaten down at least a little. If he stands firm, though, you'll have to accept that he knows that even if you won't buy at that price, someone else will. Dress shops usually price the stock, but are susceptible to offers if the item has been hanging fire for several weeks, because if goods don't turn over pretty fast customers get bored with looking at the same things.

How to find   Many of the smaller shops come and go rather fast and are therefore not listed in the Yellow Pages, so it's a question of looking out for them in the streets, or hearing about them from satisfied clients. Furniture shops may be found under Secondhand Dealers.

Street markets

Of all the various ways to shop for secondhand goods, strolling through a street market on a fine sunny morning is one of the most pleasant. A lively market in a big city has everything: chattering cosmopolitan crowds, stallholders with strong lines in comic patter, fresh air and an exciting atmosphere. Goods on offer may be anything from genuine antiques to reject china, nuts and bolts, vacuum cleaner spares, Italian shoes, bolts of cloth and exotic fruit and vegetables. But just because they are so entertaining many street markets have become tourist attractions, which means goodbye to any hope of bargains.

London has so many street markets that whole books have

been written about them. Perhaps the best known of all is in the Portobello Road, which runs from Notting Hill Gate right up to Westbourne Park Road. The southern end is very smart and prices are high, particularly during the summer when tourists are thick on the ground. But as you go further north things get junkier and junkier, and prices lower and lower. Portobello is a Saturday market, although the shops alongside are open normal hours.

Camden Passage in Islington is *all* smart. It deals solely in antiques (even the clothing is antique – Victorian shifts and the like – and ethnic items). There are a lot of shops crammed into a short pedestrian precinct, plus stalls on Wednesdays and Saturdays, and a number of arcades off the main drag. For me, Camden Passage is a place to go for *looking*, to get your eye in for the sort of things you then hope to spot at a quarter the price in other places.

Equally famous, but entirely different, is Bermondsey Market in south London. Its real name is the New Caledonian Market, but it is always called after the square in which it takes place. This is a dealers' market devoted to antiques and operates on Friday mornings, starting about 5 o'clock. (This is to put off tourists and you and me.) At Bermondsey dealers buy the stuff which they then resell several times to each other before it finally reaches some innocent member of the public who may pay ten times what was originally asked. So if you can face getting up so early (remember, for most of the year it will still be dark, so take a torch) you might well find some bargains. Or you might fall prey to a sharp stall holder (and there is no other kind in Bermondsey, or anywhere else for that matter) who spots you at a glance as an outsider and raises the price by 100 per cent. Nor is there much chance of finding some unrecognised little treasure; in Bermondsey they know the price of everything *and* the value of everything.

If you stagger out to Bermondsey take the opportunity of going on to the Salvation Army's place in Spa Road nearby, where there are many things for sale including a large selection of furniture. (But they don't open until 10 o'clock. Never mind, Bermondsey has plenty of hot dog, tea and coffee stalls to keep bleary-eyed dealers going.)

For actually buying things lesser markets are usually a better proposition for the likes of you and me. London has a great many, and most big towns have at least one. Some are well established, others come and go; some specialise and some are general.

Bargaining over prices is the done thing at all markets. The stallholder expects it and would despise you if you didn't; *you* would be foolish not to try. For the pick of the day's offerings go early; for bargain prices go late when they are packing up. On the whole it's best not to buy at markets anything that functions, and is therefore likely not to, as you may never even be able to find that particular stall holder again, let alone get any money back. And always keep a tight hold on your purse or wallet in the jostling crowds; not all those lovely people are shoppers or tourists.

How to find Any tourist guide should include the local markets, with the days they operate. But it's often difficult to find out exactly what a particular market sells without visiting it.

SOME POSSIBLE PESTS

Booklice These may turn up in old books but are harmless and will disappear if the books are kept warm and dry.

Carpet beetles If you see a little beetle like a mottled ladybird ambling around on your carpet put it outside quick. There it will just feast on flower nectar; indoors it will produce eggs and furry larvae known as woolly bears that are more voracious than any clothes moths. Signs of woolly bear attacks are rows of little holes along seams of fabric or edges of carpets. Cure: vacuum clean all fluff and debris from neglected corners everywhere; spray affected items with carpet beetle killer or mothproofer.

Clothes moths Moth larvae do not like man-made fibre, so we have rather lost the habit of protecting garments from them. But secondhand clothes are more likely to be made of natural fibres which they love, particularly wool; and they are very partial to fur coats too. They also prefer dirty clothes to clean ones. So make sure all secondhand textiles are washed or dry cleaned, and take the good old-fashioned precaution of placing moth repellant discs or strips in chests and wardrobes (they don't smell nasty these days). Spray upholstery with mothproofer.

Fleas If you find yourself afflicted with large, itchy skin bumps, fleas are around. These are most likely to be cat fleas, imported in the dormant stage in some comfy item of furniture regularly used by somebody's moggy, and a few bites are nothing to panic about. First give the item a good clean, then spray thoroughly with long-lasting insecticide. Another way of putting paid to fleas is to hang up a long-term anti-fly block.

Mites A tiny speck of dust that suddenly gets up and walks away is a furniture mite. An old sofa stuffed with vegetable fibres and coming from damp conditions can be heavily infested with these. But the cure is simple – turn up the heating as high as possible for an hour or two, and thoroughly dry and air the furniture. Spraying with long-lasting insecticide will help too.

House dust mites are barely visible to the naked eye, and are present in every home in beds and bedding. They are harmless to most people, but some are allergic to them, and they don't do asthmatics any good. Keep them down by regular vacuuming of matresses and airing of bedding; use dust-free foam-filled pillows.

Woodworm Last but most dangerous. Inspect everything you buy (wicker baskets and treen as well as furniture) for signs of the woodworm: small, neat round holes, often in the *backs* of chests and cupboards. Sometimes little piles of fine sawdust will appear on the floor. Never leave it untreated, however minor or dead it appears. It may well still be alive and could quietly spread into your house timbers. Buy a woodworm-killing fluid and an injector bottle. Coat *all* surfaces of the item with the fluid, and inject it into the holes – treat them at about 5cm (2in) intervals if numerous, as they interconnect inside. The fluid is slightly oily but dries out after a week or two. Untouched furniture can be protected from attack by polishing with an insecticidal polish, putting the first application on all surfaces.

YOUR LEGAL RIGHTS

The Sale of Goods Act 1979 gives you the same rights when buying goods secondhand as when buying new, provided they come from a dealer. It does not cover buying from private individuals or at an auction, except in so far as any description given must be accurate.

The basic provision of this Act, which is a civil law of contract, is that goods must be of merchantable quality, which means fit to perform whatever task they were made for – a washing machine must wash, a kettle must hold water. But of course the law takes into account the price paid for a secondhand article, and its age; it cannot be expected to perform as well as a brand new one, or to be in perfect condition. Always ask lots of direct questions, and if you don't get satisfactory replies, don't buy. The answer to 'Does it work?' must be 'Yes', not 'I think so, guv'! Sometimes of course dealers may not necessarily know whether a garment is real silk, or how old an appliance is. But if they make any specific claims these must be true, or they are in breach of a criminal law, the Trades Descriptions Act. It's up to you to inspect things closely, find the faults for yourself, test if possible/applicable and make your own decisions about quality.

Under the Consumer Safety Act of 1978 and Consumer Protection Act of 1961, it is an offence for a dealer to sell certain possibly dangerous goods. (Again, private sales and auctions are excluded). These are goods for which certain safety standards have been laid down, and inevitably many secondhand ones do not comply. The Acts cover oil heaters and lamps; fireguards; prams, pushchairs and carrycot stands; nightdresses, children's hood fastenings and toys; a range of electrical equipment including electric blankets; and some cooking utensils. Electrical equipment also automatically falls foul of the later Act if it has flex in the old wiring colours (red, black and green).

But of course substandard electrical equipment is in use all over the country; it only becomes illegal when sold. So the law is broken every day. *You* won't be prosecuted for buying, only the dealer for selling, so you don't have to worry about that. What you should worry about is whether the possible risks outweigh the saving in money. In certain cases – like electric blankets, or any products for the use of children or old people – obviously they do not.

Private sales
If you buy something privately from a person in his own home the law does not give you much protection. The description given in a classified ad or on a newsagent's notice board must be accurate. But the role about merchantable quality does not apply. The seller is not obliged to reveal any defects, however serious; it is up to you to find out. So once again, ask lots of questions and test wherever you can. The average person shies away from telling a direct lie, so evasive answers should make you wary. But a real villain will have no qualms about telling a thumper with a convincing smile. So don't take too much notice of what you are told – use your eyes, and the results of any testing, to decide whether to buy and what to pay.

Another hazard is the so-called private person who is

actually a dealer. A lot of shady dealers use classified ads and pretend to be private individuals to escape the strictures of the various Acts. The law has clamped down on this by insisting that dealers so declare themselves, but you may still notice some operating in this way. Look out for repetitions of the same phone number, usually offering the same sort of items.

Note: Jumble sales and charity shops are not, as is sometimes supposed, private sales.

Auctions

An auctioneers' conditions of sale usually try to take away all your legal rights, and leave you buying at your own risk. They should always be available for study, either in the catalogue or elsewhere.

Goods are only briefly described in the catalogue. This description should be accurate, but will give no indication of any flaws, except sometimes the addition of the letters a.f. (as found). Auctioneers do not intend to deceive, but obviously they cannot be familiar with the hundreds of articles passing through their hands. Thorough inspection of the goods on viewing day is essential. About the only grounds for returning anything to an auction room are cases where a work of art subsequently proves to be a forgery, or a hallmarked item is wrongly described. But if you can convince an auctioneer that you have good reason for complaint he would probably, for the sake of his own reputation, put it back into the next auction for you. You might even end up making a profit!

Stolen goods

Some people are nervous of buying secondhand goods because of the risk that they may have been stolen. The law is clear on this: if you bought in good faith and had no reason to suspect wrong-doing you will not be prosecuted for handling stolen goods. Jewellery and other small valuables are the most likely secondhand items to have been stolen. There is no reason why you should suspect even the most dingy-looking shop or market stall; but the man who sidles up to you in a pub, or roving street pedlars, are another matter. Also, if the thief is brought to book, and goods traced to you through the address on a cheque, you might have to give them back to the rightful owner.

Returning faulty goods

Some shops used to display notices saying No Money Refunded, but these are now illegal and you can report the trader to your Trading Standards Department. Nor is it essential to have a receipt, althouth this is useful as a record of the date on which the transaction took place, and between whom. Should you have cause to return badly defective goods it prevents a dealer from claiming either that you have had them for many months or that you did not buy from him in the first place. You will notice that few dealers issue receipts; you'll have to ask. Paying by cheque is another method of recording the deal . . . you will also find that dealers prefer cash, even though a cheque backed by a banker's card is just as good for sums up to £50. He has his reasons for this, the Inland Revenue being one of them, but will usually take a cheque rather than lose a sale.

If you have studied this book thoroughly you should rarely need to return goods. But if you do get landed with something flawed in some way that could not be spotted at the time, or that was wrongly described, you are legally entitled to get your money back. Whether you will actually succeed in doing so is another matter. A dealer is naturally reluctant to return hard cash. He may offer a repair, which could well be the answer. Credit notes are by no means a good substitute for cash. Accepting one means you forgo your legal rights. And as they usually have an expiry date on them, you may well find that there is nothing you want from that shop within the time set. If you are quite sure you are entitled to a refund under the law and he refuses, write him a formal letter giving the reasons and threatening court action.

Going to court is time-consuming and may cost you money. How to set about it without using a solicitor is explained in a booklet available from Citizen's Advice Bureaux and Trading Standards Departments, entitled *Small Claims in the County Court*. But note that winning your case does not magically get the money out of a reluctant or penniless dealer.

USEFUL ADDRESSES

The Art Veneer Company
Industrial Estate
Mildenhall, IP28 7AY
*Veneers, clock movements and
dials, period brassware;
mail order catalogue*

J.D. Beardmore & Co. Ltd
3 Percy Street
London W1P 0EJ
*Large range of period door and
window furniture*

CoSIRA (Council for Small
Industries in Rural Areas)
141 Castle Street
Salisbury SP1 3TP
Addresses of local craftsmen

Dry Cleaning
Information Bureau
178 Great Portland Street
London W1N 6AQ

Dylon International
Consumer Advice Bureau
Worsley Bridge Road
London SE26 5HD
*Free advice on stain removal
and dyeing*

The Eaton Bag Co. Ltd
16 Manette Street
London W1V 5LB
*Grass cloth, rattan, bamboo
and cane; send s.a.e. for list
and samples*

Ellis Stykes & Co. Ltd
Victoria Works
Howeard Street
Stockport, Cheshire
*Suppliers of parts for old Godin
stoves*

The Handicraft Shop
47 Northgate
Canterbury, Kent
*Suppliers of handicraft
materials; mail order catalogue*

W. Hobby Ltd
Knights Hill Square
London SE27 0HH
*Clock movements, faces and
hands, also veneers; mail order
catalogue*

Glass & Glazing Federation
6 Mount Row
London W1
*Addresses of stained and leaded
glass repairers*

The Lighter & Shaver
Repair Centre
231 Oxford Street
London W1

Renubath Services (London)
596 Chiswick High Road
London W4 5RS
Old baths re-enamelled

Sander & Kay Ltd
170 Cricklewood Broadway
London NW2
Government surplus clothing;
mail order catalogue

Solid Fuel Advisory Service
Hobart House
Grosvenor Place
London SW1 7AE
Free advice on installing old
fireplaces

Suede Services Ltd
2a Hoop Lane
Golders Green Road
London NW11
Leather and suede garments
restored and cleaned; postal
service

Christopher Wray
600 King's Road
London SW6
Spare parts for old light fittings;
wide range of reconditioned
fittings

FURTHER READING

The Antique Collector's Guide David Benedictus, Macmillan 1980
Antique Furniture (Teach Yourself Book) Ernle Bradford,
E.U.P. 1970
Antiques from the Victorian Home Bea Howe, Batsford 1973
Art Deco of the 20s and 30s Bevis Hillier, Studio Vista 1968
Better than New – a practical guide to renovating furniture Albert
Jackson and David Day, BBC Publications 1982
Bevis Hillier's Pocket Guide to Antiques Mitchell Beazley 1981
Collecting Now: Care and Repair of Your Antiques John FitzMaurice
Mills, BBC 1982
Country Furniture Jane Toller, David & Charles 1973
The Country Life Collector's Pocket Book of Silver Judith Banister,
Country Life Books 1982
English Silver Hall Marks ed. Judith Banister, Foulsham 1983
A Guide to Collecting Silver, Elizabeth de Castres/J.Goddard & Sons
Ltd, Queen Anne Press 1980
How to Restore and Repair Practically Everything Lorraine Johnson,
Nelson 1978
London Street Markets Kevin Perlmutter, Wildwood House 1983
The Lyle Official Antiques Review Lyle Publications, annual
The Markets of London Alec Forshaw and Theo Bergström,
Penguin 1983
Searching for Antiques Jane Toller, Ward Lock 1970
The Story of English Furniture Bernard Price, Ariel Books 1982
Victoriana James Laver, Ward Lock 1973 (revised ed)
Victoriana Collector's Handbook Charles Platten Woodhouse,
Bell 1970